Do not fear in
heart. God is

L. Craig Rikard

Hidden Epidemic

Mabel,

What great memories we
share! Your faithfulness
to Ebenezer has always
touched me. May you
always stay in touch.
May this book help someone
God places in your path.

Craig

Tiger Iron Press
Macon, Georgia, USA

Hidden Epidemic

D. Craig Rikard

Tiger Iron Press

Cover design by Julianne Gleaton, see www.juliannedesign.com

Includes resources and suggestions for reading, and pictures. Printed in the United States of America.

ISBN-13: 978-0-9787263-5-5

Search for: addiction; children of the addicted; suicide; what an addicted mother can do to the unborn; bipolar disease; getting help for families where addiction exists; new facilities for children of addicted parents; mental problems; children's mental problems; hope for a family where addiction exists.

First Edition: September, 2010

Dedication

Jenny Dell Rikard
Jan. 31, 1956 - May 27, 2008

This book is dedicated in loving memory to my sister, Jenny Dell Rikard, one of the most courageous people in my life. Her story provides all of us with a song of hope, softly and sweetly sung beneath the discord of life's chaos. Few could sing it better than Jenny.

Table of Contents

PART III
THE FINISH OR THE START?

PART IV
ADDITIONS

Introduction

Although many books deal with the problem of addiction – how to get help, the harm it can do, and useful treatments – few books discuss the tragic implications for the children of addicted parents, particularly young children. Yet these children can be robbed of their childhoods, isolated, abused, confused as to what is happening, and deprived of their own feelings of self-esteem and worth. In fact, the child of an addicted parent may grow up with more difficulties and hidden wounds than the addicted parent. *Hidden Epidemic* deals with just such children and points out the pervasiveness of this problem, and what to do about it.

Dr. Craig Rikard is supremely qualified to tackle this secret epidemic not only because as a therapist and minister, he treats many families in which such children grow up, but also because his sister and he were raised as the children of an addicted mother. His story is not only one of medicine, therapy, psychology and prayer. It is also the very personal story of his own childhood living in a pretty home in suburbia, where no one could hear the screams, slaps, and abusive language. As Dr. Rikard so aptly points out, children of addiction come from every socio-economic section of the United States. The pusher does not need to sell his wares in wealthier areas; the unintended loopholes in our prescription system can also amply satisfy the desire for mood-altering, addictive drugs. Furthermore, scientific surveys prove that the plight of these children is now an epidemic, however hidden it may be.

In spite of such a serious subject, the book is fascinating, the journey hard, and yet there is hope and light for those caught within the grasp of addictive parents or caretakers. Dr. Rikard shows the reader specific difficulties and symptoms that children of an addicted caretaker may have; how to take steps to remedy the situation; and how to get help for those who need it. Most of all Rikard demonstrates that there is hope – both for the children and the addicts. We need more books such as this one. We can no longer afford to ignore its implications.

A. Louise Staman, Editor
Tiger Iron Press

PART ONE

THE HIDDEN VICTIMS

Chapter 1

One Big Happy Family

"Hey Jenny. How Are You?"

Gail, my spouse of thirty-five years, stirred the Christmas boil on the stove. The aroma from the mixture in the pot filled the house with smells of cinnamon, apples, and evergreen. We loved Christmas and all its trappings. The sights, smells and sounds that touched the senses from Thanksgiving to Christmas Day filled me with wonder and sadness. Though some of my memories from childhood were painful, the passing years enabled my family to create its own traditions. These new traditions reinvigorated the season of Christmas and allowed me to push the painful memories into a place somewhere deep in the soul, out of the way. Those memories remained safely tucked away and liberated me to enjoy this beautiful season, that is, until Jenny arrived for our family Christmas.

Dad and Mom raised three children. Only two years of age separated Jenny and me. Penny, on the other hand, was a surprise baby. She arrived twelve years after my birth. Therefore, Jenny and I shared a childhood unknown to Penny. The experiences Jenny and I shared Penny never witnessed; for that I remain thankful.

For the last ten years my entire family gathered at our parsonage for Christmas Day. We circled a tree Gail and I decorated with great care. It always seemed to possess a perfect symmetry. Large ornaments hung from the longer lower limbs, growing smaller toward the top as did the branches. A beautiful angel with wings unfolded topped the tree. Candles were lit and along with the white lights of the tree provided that aura I liked to call the Christmas glow. Beneath the tree were mounds of gifts carefully wrapped.

Like one of Rockwell's artistic expressions of Christmas, we gathered around the tree to exchange gifts. Laughter and commentary filled the air as we "ooed" and "ahhed" over every gift. Each gift was opened one at a time with all watching. There was no mass rush to grab gifts and tear the wrapping away. The process was slow, deliberate and delightful. The only tension anyone might notice would have been the unrestrained excitement and childlike exuberance.

However, a powerful tension crackled between Jenny and me like damaged electrical wire with the worn places touching and sparking. Jenny and I shared exposed wounds from childhood; yet they remained unseen by everyone in the circle. This year the current of stress moving between us was taking on greater power. It was almost too strong to control. The moments when our anxiety moved to the surface amid our family merriment and sparked were becoming more frequent. Thankfully, Jenny and I managed to hide the potent distress stirring in our relationship; but we recognized it and acutely felt it.

In earlier years we could hide our personal discomfort with overcompensation. We could laugh loudest and talk the most. This year it was now difficult to laugh, and though talking with others presented us with little difficulty, we strained to converse as brother and sister. The sparks were becoming noticeable. Our glances toward one another were little more than a rapid meeting of the eyes before looking elsewhere. Our conversation was always stilted and shallow; even our laughter sounded contrived and forced. Still, our family never sensed the severity of the shared tension making Jenny and me fidget, rise from our chairs to pace a little, then sit down to fight the nervous energy again.

The passing years had been unkind to Jenny and me physically. We both suffered severe damage to the lower back; therefore rising and moving about would have been understandable and acceptable to the other family members. I am certain no one gave our nervous tics and anxious expressions another thought. How much longer we could continue the pretense that all was well remained to be seen.

We had every reason, so I believed, to enjoy the company of the other. Jenny was a trained nurse, and a good one. Having won nurse of the month on several occasions at the hospital she served, Jenny enjoyed a reputation for genuine caring. When a car accident damaged my spine, leading to six surgeries, Jenny was my nurse and painstakingly cared for me. She nursed me as though she cared for the most important person in the world. Her passion for my welfare was admirably demonstrated when the insurance company demanded I go home following the fifth surgery after only two days in the hospital. Jenny heard the news, then without comment ran down the hall and called the doctor. A roustabout with the insurance company ensued and Jenny, with the help of the doctor, won. I heard of Jenny's over-and-above style of nursing from others; now I was the recipient of her compassion.

I cared for Jenny just as passionately, but differently. I worried about her as a parent worries for a child. Jenny developed a severe case of bipolar illness in adulthood. I was powerless in all attempts to help her with this struggle, so like a parent, I worried about her and prayed for her. Jenny looked up to me as a parental figure, and in times of crisis always called me and wanted my opinion. She needed to hear me say her current battles were going to be okay. Though I often had no answers, just affirming she would survive meant the world to her.

We had every reason to sit together in a room, laugh freely and just talk as two siblings who loved the company of the other. But, we couldn't. There was another force, a dark entity more powerful than our mutual love and care. Although I had been a clergyman for more than thirty years, and also an educated family therapist, I could not talk about the restlessness percolating in my soul with Jenny. She was just as incapable. That particular Christmas I began to realize why the painful childhood we experienced was now snaking its way upward from that dark place I considered a safe place of storage. We were growing weak. As we age we grow more sentimental and struggle to control our emotions. The emotional life Jenny and I shared was potent, and as two midlife adults we battled to keep that life confined deeply within ourselves.

As I looked across the room at Jenny I realized I had been far more successful suppressing that past. The only vulnerability I felt regarding its ability to affect my present life was when Jenny was around. Jenny was the reminder of all I wanted to forget. Consequently, though I loved her dearly, I could not draw near to her heart. The more intimately we talked, the greater my awareness of that painful childhood we shared. My sitting across the room from her was its own metaphor, for that is the way we lived; we looked across an insidious dark abyss at one another, afraid to move forward in our relationship. Too many steps forward and we would be standing in that agonizing darkness called the past.

As a minister and counselor I am certain many families share painful experiences. They sit around tables, Christmas trees, or stand and talk at get-togethers while never mentioning the past. This is a shallow interaction at best. Like most of us with painful pasts, avoidance is our method of choice in dealing with it, or not dealing with it. They will continue to live, as Jenny and I, looking at one another from an emotional distance. They will love and care about one another, but the pain of their yesterdays will not allow them to touch emotionally. In reality, a painful past can never keep us apart unless we allow it to do so. We are just too afraid of experiencing the sting of that pain again. We live in emotional distance, saying little, meaning little in what we do say, and hoping one day things will get better. Like me, many will remain clueless as to how the relationships will improve; we just hope they will. What a momentous mistake.

I looked again at Jenny. The severe pain of her childhood had taken its toll on her body. At almost fifty years of age she looked old. Her weight loss was so substantial she looked like a stick, her face too thin and drawn. Her eyes and teeth looked as though they were now too big for her withering frame. I felt a tinge of nausea in the pit of my stomach. I knew more than anyone the cause of the vicious wear and tear on her body. I could only imagine how tattered was her soul.

A memory rushed to mind that Christmas, a recollection that allowed me to chuckle to myself even amid the painful observations I was making. Jenny was about three or four years of age. She was a delightful child, a "look at me" child who engaged in some of the oddest and funniest behaviors to gain attention. She always found a way to amuse me and others, even at risk of getting in trouble. One evening Mom drove us to the local bus station to pick up a family member arriving in town. Jenny noticed the stairs and could not resist seeing where they led. The stair railing consisted of metal bars several inches apart, supporting the handrail. Jenny decided to see if her head would fit between the bars. It did. "Mama, look at me! Look Craig!" Her little face smiled as she looked at the gathering crowd below her. As she attempted to pull her head out, the bars seemed to have closed. Whereas most children would panic and cry, Jenny found it delightful. The attention she merited that night was worth the trouble to her. The fire department had to send two firemen, in uniform at that, to remove Jenny's head from between the rails. Once her head slipped through, she stood and smiled at the crowd. Our red-faced mother did not consider the matter funny. However, Jenny had a story to tell for weeks. This was only one of many such moments when Jenny delighted us.

As I sat in reflection of that moment, strangely, a song resonated in my head. We were a family who loved music. As a matter of fact, we learned to find solace and escape in and through popular music. One summer, when Mom's behavior was growing more erratic, I allowed myself to become lost in my own created world. As a Beatle fan I wore a fuzzy black hair ball sold as a

"Beatle Wig," and pretended to be Paul McCartney the entire summer. I knew every Beatle song by heart. All of the pictures I owned of The Beatles showed them wearing long trousers. That summer I refused to wear shorts. I roasted in the South Georgia heat as I role-played. The life of a Beatle appeared to possess none of the painful events occurring in our house. Today those same songs bring great joy to my life.

Jenny on the other hand had claimed "Georgie Girl" as her song. We often heard her singing it around our small lower-middle class home, off key of course. The song got on Mom's nerves, but I liked hearing her belt it out. In later years the song would almost become prophetic for Jenny.

That Christmas I realized the music stopped years ago for Jenny. She was no longer singing, but rather living the lyrics of "Georgie Girl." "Nobody you meet could ever see the loneliness there." But I did. Anyone who took the time to look into Jenny's eyes, notice the physical alterations, and listen to her lifeless dialogues, could discern a very lonely person.

Chapter 2

Families and Substance Abuse

"Were We The Only Ones?"

When most Americans are asked to describe their images of drug addiction, they portray a person living on the street. For us the addict wears dated and tattered clothing or even second-hand clothing discovered in a dumpster. We assume most are out of touch with their families. Either the family has disowned them, or they have become so disoriented from their drug use, they no longer care about going home. Some picture the addict with a new family, a family of the street. They live beneath bridges, in empty buildings, or crash at any house or shelter that welcomes them. The neighborhood where they live is dark and desolate. The rundown buildings almost mimic the bodies of the addicts that walk their streets. The outer structure of the buildings and the body of the addict show the wear and tear of abuse and neglect. This is the addict common in films and documentaries. Sadly, many of these images are accurate.

Now picture a suburban home housing a common nuclear family. There is a father, mother and two to three children. The father works, sometimes along with the mother. Some mothers choose to rear their children at home as their work. The outside of their home looks much like the other houses in the neighborhood. If we knock on the door, a smiling adult or curious child greets us. If we enter for a visit, we notice a clean orderly house. The mother and father are kind and engage in conversations that are comfortable and put us at ease. Upon leaving we think, "They are a nice normal family."

Unknown and hidden to us is the fact of the mother's addiction to prescription drugs. She has learned to muster the strength and skills necessary to fool us. Yet, as soon as we leave, her actions can turn unpredictable and erratic. The father is a kind, caring man, but his energies are devoted to enabling his wife and mother of his children. The smiling children who appeared so well-behaved sat in our presence in terror of saying the wrong thing during our visit. We didn't notice they were a little too quiet. It was more natural to assume they were just well-behaved.

Within a matter of hours the peaceful normal home we visited can erupt into an abusive and violent place. The family lives under one roof, but its relationships are strained. An emotional desolation is present, and if we visited often over several years, we would witness the abuse and neglect responsible for the fading smiles and forced expressions of joy. An addict lives in the home, and all dwelling inside feel isolated and lonely. There exists an inner cold as though they dwelt beneath a bridge. Though they are family members, the presence of drug abuse has almost made the inhabitants strangers to one another, like those in a shelter unacquainted with the person sleeping on the next cot.

Drug addiction is as common in suburban America as it is in the inner city. The neighborhood streets of America's small towns can house men, women and youth as strongly addicted to drugs as abandoned buildings in deserted areas of larger cities. Of course, there are few pushers of narcotics and other mood-altering drugs, for they are not needed. The ones addicted to drugs can acquire their medications with prescriptions. They have learned to manipulate doctors and how to squeeze through the loop holes present in the methods pharmacies use to dispense the drugs.

The consequence of addiction is the same, always the same, whether one lives in an environment of dark decaying streets, or one that real estate agents tout as a fine neighborhood with good schools. Every addict journeys downward into the depths of emotional despair and eventually death unless intervention occurs. Loving family members join them on the destructive journey.

The discomfort and agony Jenny and I felt that Christmas was birthed through years of abusive words and events occurring in a home that appeared normal. Even though life within the house grew severely chaotic and destructive over time, most outsiders remained unaware of this painful existence. Through silence and fear we hid the destructive effects of our mother's substance abuse behind the doors and walls of our home.

Prescription drug abuse is a major problem in American culture. Fathers and mothers parenting young children in middle-class America can be as addicted to drugs as the user waiting on the street corner for his supplier to arrive. In many of these homes children live in unimaginable pain. If you are a parent caught within the web of substance abuse and are convinced your children remain unaffected, Jenny and I want to strongly warn you, *"It is not so!"* We also issue a plea to those institutions designed to treat drug addiction, "Please, do not forget the small children." Never assume they are too young to feel the chaos and notice the subtle changes occurring in the life of their mother or father. Finally, we offer a wake-up call to caring individuals, especially to those living in middle and upper-class America. There is a high probability children like Jenny and me live in your neighborhood.

In a survey conducted in 2001 by SAMSHA, a government-sponsored web page on substance abuse, six million children lived in a home with at least one parent abusing drugs. According to a recent study by the National Survey on Drug Abuse and Health, that number has increased to eight million. Thirteen percent of these children were eleven years of age and under.

These numbers should alarm every reader. The possibility one of these children lives within our reach is extremely high; they need our help. Statistics reveal that the intervention of a caring adult "from the outside" makes a positive difference.

Why do so many small children remain unknown? Remember, like Jenny and me, most of these children are taught to live in silence regarding their home life. Therefore, their number is actually higher and our exposure to their needs even greater. As Doug Larson said, "Children are often the silent victims of drug abuse." We are the hidden epidemic.

PART II

OUR STORY

Chapter 3

Questions Without Answers

"I Didn't Know What to Do"

Dad finally spoke, breaking the uneasy silence. I had no idea when I accompanied him to the back porch that he would validate over forty years of powerful, uncomfortable feelings. His memories also affirmed the accuracy of my own. Most importantly he finally addressed many of the unanswered questions and disconnected events from my childhood. He raised his head and began, "Craig, I'm so sorry."

Few men delighted in their backyard like Dad. Every afternoon he and my stepmother Gladys sat on a wooden deck in two weathered patio chairs. Although the deck was rather cluttered, the yard was immaculately manicured. Only the most inclement weather forced them to cancel that afternoon appointment of sitting outside. Bird houses and feeders hung from limbs here and there, and Marlin gourds adorned metal poles, housing over a dozen birds. On the far right side of the yard grew his garden, which this year was thriving. The air smelled of charcoal and honeysuckle. The old grill appeared rusted, but remained well used. Rarely did I visit without dining on grilled ribs. The long fence marking the rear of the yard was thick with honeysuckle vines. The yard expressed my father's personality more articulately than any verbal description I could offer. His soul was anchored in the fertile soil; his delight soared with every plant that sprouted and flowered; and the sense of usefulness he needed in his retirement was visible in the care with which he tended the yard and everything within its bounds.

He always invited me to join him on the porch. To Dad it was a despicable act to prop oneself in a recliner in front of a television on a beautiful day. I learned from my father to love the late afternoon; early in adulthood it became my favorite time of day. Sitting with him was like watching the earth yawn as creation seemed to slow; the shadows reminded me of someone slowly pulling a blanket over the yard as everything there prepared for sleep. Late afternoon is poetry; those few hours are filled with enough symbolism to fill a heart with wonder and serenity.

Since his marriage to Gladys, Dad and I had become good friends. Our relationship now thrived. I was emotionally closer to my father those last years than at any time in our shared history. During most visits he bragged about his garden and shared his newly acquired knowledge from the latest addition of the *Almanac*. It was almost a sacred book to him.

However, today he was unusually quiet. Two years earlier he had a religious experience that transformed his life. He stepped forward, alone and unexpectedly, in a local church and chose to follow Christ. Even Gladys was surprised by his decision. As a clergyman for thirty years I recalled no Christian decision more sincere than Dad's. Publicly stepping out alone to make such a personal decision contradicted everything that defined his personality. He loved quiet solitude, and kept his most serious thoughts and feelings to himself. A fresh openness followed that decision, and sharing from the heart became a beautiful, welcomed attribute of his life. His words and mannerisms were now adorned with a touching tenderness. Over the last years I never greeted or left him without a kiss to the cheek and the words, "I love you." He always reciprocated.

Sitting on the porch that late afternoon I intuitively felt he was wrestling with strong emotions. When he faced me, he appeared uncomfortable, as though he feared speaking. From his body language it was obvious he needed to reveal something that was disturbing him. Dad proceeded to reveal the most important story I needed to hear from my father. He steadied himself emotionally, squeezed the arms of the chair and offered me the honest, detailed story of my childhood. Few stones, if any, were left unturned.

For most of my adult life I suffered from a powerful sense of incompleteness. My childhood years were filled with unanswered questions and mystifying events. Instinctively I knew my wholeness and serenity had everything to do with understanding those years. Through observations and conversations here and there I pieced together a measure of understanding regarding what happened in those early years and why. Visiting with Dad affirmed my fear that in spite of what I knew, I was still looking into a dark shadowy past consisting of many unanswered questions and mystifying events.

Questions raced through my mind as I sat there. Why was the past so frightening to me? Why did I experience confusion when attempting to describe my childhood? What actually happened around us, unseen and unheard in those years? These represented the tip of the iceberg of unanswered questions for which I needed answers. My attempt to understand the past was like playing with one of those *connect the dots* puzzles we used in elementary school. However, the dots comprising my childhood were often far apart, and many seemed missing. From my perspective, developing an integrated picture of my childhood appeared impossible. Consequently, self-confidence and serenity would remain elusive until questions were answered, the truth confronted and the mystery dispelled. Dad was about to open the door into the liberating truth.

Dad also suffered during those years. When he chose to open that door, he dared to face his own imperfections, accomplishments and failures. I will forever be thankful to God for Dad's transformed life, the tenderness that redefined and refined his life, and for his courage in facing a painful past with his son. Nervously he looked at me and in essence said, "Come, walk with me."

That afternoon with my father was related to his need for reconciliation; still, it was very much about me. In the end, that afternoon was the gift of truth from a father to his son. For the first time I began to truly understand who I was and why I felt as I did. However, I had no premonition concerning the severity of the events that would unfold over the next few years. I did not know that I would revisit the past again as the approaching years passed. The past would no longer be about my need for personal self-discovery and emotional completeness. It would be related to an issue far graver to me. I would need to revisit the past for closure.

Only God and I would "sit on the porch" this time. Now I needed the past to help me find meaning and hope amid the worst suffering in my life. Without that afternoon with Dad I would be staring into a piecemeal past, searching for traces of truth and light here and there; but Dad's courageous revelation lifted much of the mysterious veil. How could the painful childhood Dad and I shared that afternoon help bring closure, meaning and hope? The childhood we shared was above all things true. Yes, it was painful, but it was true. Truth is liberating and a gift from God. Where there is truth, there is always light.

On this occasion I was looking for light and hope, and that light existed somewhere in the truth of the story we shared that day. With God I would visit those stories again and find that light. Only then could meaning emerge, and hope appear. I began to converse with my departed father in my heart: "Dad, you never knew what was coming, but you prepared me for it by choosing to be honest and truthful with your son. Now, I pray the truth will indeed set me free. I am devastated, and I need liberation from the pain and meaninglessness overwhelming me. I need some means of rising above the powerful regret I feel. Dad, God and I are going to sit on your back porch for awhile."

"Mama, Why Are You Not Like You Used to Be?"

"Mama, you used to love going places. We almost always visited friends and ate meals with them. I remember driving around at Christmas and looking at all the lights. We laughed looking in store windows. Jenny and I loved Christmas mornings. Everyone was happy. You always smiled when you got your presents. We also particularly liked swimming with you in the summer. You swam with us and played in the water. Now you just lie around, Mama. You don't want to leave the house anymore, and we don't see our friends either. Are they still friends with you and Daddy? Are you so sick you don't feel like talking to them? We are afraid to wake you, but we don't know what to do when you sleep on the sofa so much of the day. You don't smile much anymore. We know you must hurt because we hear you tell Daddy about what's hurting you. It always seems like he's sitting at the kitchen table trying to pay bills. Now you are sick all the time, and Daddy spends all the time taking care of you. Are you ever going to get well again?"

How do you explain a mother's drug addiction and its upsetting behaviors to her children? Is there any means to explain the erratic, unpredictable, ever-changing personality so that her young children might understand the profound changes occurring in her life? The answer is an emphatic "No!" Should someone try? From the heart I cry, "Yes!" Jenny and I lived in a world of laughter, screams and silence. Laughter, we understood; the screams and cold silence terrified and mystified us. We needed a word that assured and comforted.

In the early years of our childhood our mother laughed and enjoyed life. Around twenty years ago I met some of my mother's high school friends, and those who knew her in the young adult years. From birth until marriage Mom lived in a small Alabama town. Everyone either knew most of the residents, or they were related to them. They described her as popular, active, delightfully on-the-go, joyful and kind. Though she experienced an emotional break at age twelve and was already addicted to drugs prior to giving birth to me, Mom's friends described a very different woman from the mother we knew in the formative years of childhood. Jenny and I perceived glimpses of the person beloved and enjoyed by her friends. As a matter of fact, when her drug use created euphoria, without the heavy sedation in those early years, our mother seemed like most other mothers we observed. Prior to her speech growing slurred and at times illogical, she was an energetic happy wife and mother.

She was an attractive woman and took great care regarding her appearance. As a young boy I thought she was the most beautiful woman in the world; but then again, most children perceive their mother in this manner. Her smile was most memorable and charming. Today a picture of her just after marriage stands on one of our tables. The photo validates the descriptions given by her friends and supports my earliest recollections. We spent hours at the homes of friends, visiting and cooking out. Though I was only four years of age and Jenny two, I possess strong clear memories of adventurous and playful trips.

Mom seemed most happy in the car headed anywhere, the destination seemed irrelevant. Even the most mundane trips were somehow exciting to her and thus fun for us. Jenny and I almost grew up in an area called the "Midtown Shopping Center." Though only a small collection of stores, to Jenny and me the collection of shops appeared huge. In those days Mom could leave us playing on the sidewalk for several minutes at a time. She would return to ensure that all was well and reenter the shops to browse.

In the summer months she loved to lie out in the sun. Jenny and I swam many weeks of the summer as she sunbathed. We were playmates who shared a love of the water as Mom relaxed in the sun. Every summer her skin tanned dark brown. Rarely did I ever see her sunburned. She seemed made to live in the sun. Many of the erratic outbursts that frequently occurred at home disappeared outside in the sunlight. In the sun, out of the house, Mom was at her best. She was the vivacious woman and mother not yet hidden beneath the dense fog of drug addiction. Many of the casual un-posed photographs from those earliest years are of a happy woman appearing to enjoy her life.

According to my father and others, she was on drugs even then. Drugs snare an individual by making life "feel" euphoric. Euphoria injects the user with a transient dose of energy and creates a strong pseudo self-esteem. As our mother began to consume larger doses of tranquilizers throughout our childhood, her desire to leave home to enjoy the outdoors and friends diminished. When we neared adolescence, we almost stopped leaving home altogether. When we did travel to the home of friends or to an outing, Mom's nerves began to reveal the wear and tear of the ever-shortening experience of euphoria, followed by bouts with anxiety and depression. My father later claimed that her mood at any time was related to drug use.

As the euphoria waned, Jenny and I, even as young children, began to walk on eggshells in public. Mom was often a very different person at home than in public. She expected and demanded that we guard and protect our life at home. However, she never distinguished for us the facets of our home life that were permissible to share from those forbidden. Outbursts of her anger related to something we revealed at any given time became our teacher as to what was prohibited.

Drug addicts become "homebodies" for good and sometimes illogical reasons. Thankfully, they often realize their reflexes are too slow to drive. Furthermore, they are aware that should an accident occur, they could face severe consequences if drugs are discovered in their system. Illogically, Mom often believed she needed to remain close to her stash of drugs. Dad told me that over time Mom began to think, "What if something happens while I am away, and I can't get to my medication for days?" Strange? Definitely, since we rarely ventured out of town. However, addiction quickly begins to disorient the addict and distorts reality. For example, an intoxicated or drugged driver pulled over for weaving will swear to the officer she was driving straight and safely. She becomes adamant regarding her lawful driving because in her distorted state she was driving safely. In reality she was weaving from one lane to the other. The distorted world begins to collide with reality, and over time the two become indistinguishable.

Though Jenny and I never articulated to one another the notable changes we observed in Mom's behavior and affectation, I believe we both sensed it. We had to. The mother we knew in our youngest years had life in her eyes. When she smiled, they appeared to light up. If the eyes are the windows to the soul, Mom was happy, then. However, we were watching the extinguishing of that light. Her countenance was losing its luster as a noticeable discontent began taking its place. She neglected her hair and purchased wigs she could easily slip on when needed. Her limbs atrophied and her skin turned sallow. Maintaining the appearance she once valued became a chore and was eventually neglected.

The changes in her mood were not as succinct as I make them sound. The alterations in behavior intermingled, and she slid easily and fluidly from one state of mind into another. The one factor that determined how she felt and acted at any given moment was the dosage of medication she had ingested. The air could resonate with joy, and in the twinkling of an eye it could sound dark and frightening. Jenny and I could feel approaching chaos as though it were beamed through the walls by some power that knew our mother better than we did. We could play and laugh as our mother engaged in normal maternal activities; then suddenly for unknown reasons, she could become irate and verbally abusive toward us. Therefore, as we aged we learned to play cautiously. Children forced to play in an environment of caution rather than in childish abandon begin to suffer. Jenny and I are proof of my assertion.

Again, there was a famine of explanation and understanding regarding these sudden changes in mood and behavior. As children, these contradictory words and actions were bewildering, at times striking suddenly without any explanation from anyone. A confused child is a fearful child, and therefore, never feels totally secure in life. The looming possibility that aggression could interrupt a pleasant disposition placed us on edge. Possessing some childish form of premonition that Mom's mood was growing darker was of little help. There was no secret hiding place for Jenny and me to avoid the oncoming verbal assault; and even if we hid away, our punishment would prove far more severe once found.

In our earliest childhood years Mom had far more pleasant days without angry explosive outbursts. However, with the passing months the pleasant days diminished. As a matter of fact, as Jenny entered pre-K age, the outbursts increased noticeably. Eventually, unpredictability became such a powerful dynamic we never knew what to expect from our mother. However, it was obvious that Mom was moving steadily toward anger and aggression and away from the happy pleasant mother we knew.

I still find it mystifying that Jenny and I revealed few behaviors that screamed, "We are afraid!" to the outside world. The greater possibility is that we did emotionally scream; however, Mom's ability in those early years to don a happy, maternal persona in public allowed adults to dismiss our more erratic behaviors. Over the years I have come to believe that most outside our family did not notice our fear or hear the screams of our psyches because Jenny and I learned to guard our secretive home life.

The joyful, mundane, and terrifying facets of life served as strands comprising the tapestry of our early childhood. Over time the joyful threads, and even the cords of the mundane grew frayed, much like Mom's nerves, and began to unravel. Our tapestry was slowly losing its beauty and color; by degree it was becoming a dense smothering rug that made breathing the air of childish curiosity and creativity difficult. It is not exaggeration to assert that children living within the wild mood swings of an addicted parent live a stale, stifling existence. Curiosity and creativity are the fatalities in a child's spirit when they live in fear. Children who play with one eye fearfully on their mother naturally are going to miss many of the interesting, inviting realities in life.

The most predictable dynamic in our home was the fact that Mom was sick. Thus, everyone in the house was forced to adjust to that truth or pay a high emotional price. Actually, we paid a price no matter how we responded to Mom. I emotionally suffered as she smothered me with adoration. I was anointed by her to be the favorite child. Though as a teen I lived as one desperately wanting to escape from beneath her heavy hand of favoritism, it never worked. Jenny horrendously suffered as her permanently despised victim and never escaped.

Dad recognized early in their love that there would always be another presence in the marriage: mood-altering medications. Why did he marry her, knowing their future would unfold beneath the dark cloud of addictive disease? Only Dad knew why. He possessed an illogical capacity to love. Though great instability marked our family life, and many questions remained unanswered over the years, still there was one reality Jenny and I knew beyond doubt: Dad loved Mom.

I remember the interview with Princess Diana when she addressed Prince Charles' longtime affair with Camilla Parker Bowles by saying. "It was a little crowded with three people in the marriage." Though Dad selflessly loved our mother, we had a boarder: addiction. It was no visitor; it was a resident, and Mom had no intention of paying the price to make it leave.

The tenor and tone of the house had everything to do with how Mom felt, which had everything to do with the amount of drugs taken. This vicious cycle defined our childhood. This destructive cycle was certain and predictable. Young children need certainty and predictability to feel secure. Usually, physical and emotional security is necessary for healthy development of one's self-esteem. In this case, however, predictability did nothing to create comfort and security for Jenny and me. Instead, it infected us with constant caution and fear and sharply clawed at our self-esteem.

Jenny and I learned to be "pleasing children." When studying alcoholism and substance abuse as part of my training for ministry, I learned that most families with an alcoholic spawn at least one pleasing child. This child is the peacekeeper. They attempt to keep confrontation out of the family, sometimes at great cost. Therefore, our goal was to keep Mom happy during the day so that Dad might come home to a happy place. Dad could be the recipient of the screams or silence as much as Jenny and me.

When they were at peace, Jenny and I knew a day and night of contented calm. By late childhood the scenario created by our pleasing behavior became as close to feeling "normal" as we could get.

Jenny and I felt drugs took our mother from us, and in later years we tried to understand her actions with compassion. Although this proved difficult for both of us, I admit it was easier for me than Jenny. As you continue reading of our past, you will understand why Jenny struggled to understand Mom's behavior. The intent of this book is not to say, "Look at our cruel mother!" Instead, I want the reader to catch glimpses of the mother we initially enjoyed, and possibly could have enjoyed had it not been for the drugs. Just as importantly I want you to realize how happily our family could have lived and matured.

Dad was a loving, caring man, and a good provider. He was the most selfless person I knew in my life. Jenny was hilarious and genuinely caring. She was naturally funny and lighted up any group she joined. Before her "sickness," Mom was a charming, gregarious, active woman who loved life. I was a sensitive, artistic child who was very observant of life. The characters in our family struggled to live and survive beneath the severe level of addiction that pushed us downward. Mom turned angry and slowly withdrew from life. Dad was forced to try to keep everything and everyone in the family together. Jenny struggled to maintain her God-given joy. I lost almost all confidence in myself and sought solace and meaning in music. We were losing the will to break free as individuals, and the opportunities to do so slowly vanished as drug addiction ran the family.

Though we could not understand our mother's erratic behavior, having someone attempt to explain would have been of tremendous comfort. It would have assured Jenny and me that we were not alone. We were not looking for clinical answers. We just longed for someone to explain and reassure us. In particular, we wanted to believe that our mother would one day feel better.

Lacking any form of explanation or encouragement, we did manage to find a means of escape. As stated earlier, our family was most joyful when music played in the house. Mom and Dad liked to invite neighborhood friends over and dance in the den. Jenny and I loved to watch them dance and laugh. We often joined them. Music became our best friend and a means of peace. When hiding out in our room to avoid one of Mom's bad moods, we seemed to always find a song on the radio or play a favorite record on the one turntable we owned. I believe as a boy my heart longed for the music to keep playing. As long as music played we could join the dance of life. When it stopped Jenny and I felt as though we stepped outside to watch, afraid to step in.

"Daddy, Why Does Mama Act Like She Does?"

"Daddy, I overheard that woman say Mama acted crazy. She isn't crazy is she, Daddy? I know some people look at her funny, especially when she's talking about Jenny. Why is she like she is?"

Child development specialist Virginia Satir wrote, "What lingers from the parent's individual past, unresolved or incomplete, often becomes part of her or his irrational parenting." Mom suffered from emotional distress and an appetite for mood-altering medications since age twelve. The nature of this breakdown remained a family secret, unknown to my father or us.

The emotional break was possibly related to her father's desire for a son. Farmers still needed sons as ready-made farmhands in the 1930s. My grandparents birthed one son and five girls. Their selection of the boy's name "Billy" certainly revealed the hope that my grandmother would deliver a boy. Mom was their last opportunity for a son. I can only imagine my grandfather's disappointment when the doctor entered with the announcement of their new healthy baby girl. Taking into account the farming culture of the Deep South in the years of The Great Depression, his desire for a boy and his feeling of disappointment when a daughter was born were not unusual.

As young children we knew Mom loved Granddaddy and that he was very important to her. Perhaps the event that galvanized my belief in the importance of my grandfather to Mom was Granddaddy's visits to our home. Mom was most happy when he called and informed us he was coming for a visit. These calls were rare, and Mom treated them importantly. The house was thoroughly cleaned; we were scrubbed and neatly dressed; and Mom walked about the house elated, but on edge.

Oddly, he never stayed a single night in our home. Though in those days the trip was a long, tedious drive on two-lane roads, he refused to spend the night. He and my grandmother would arise before dawn, drive all morning and arrive before noon. My grandmother was a sweet, quiet woman who never challenged Granddaddy in our presence. They would visit for three to five hours and drive home. Sadly, Mom always prepared the guest room hoping that he might change his mind. The room was immaculate. Each time my grandfather refused, and as the car drove away Mom walked into the house and wept. Jenny and I wept with her. We were not crying because our grandfather did not stay, for eventually we no longer expected him to sleep over. We cried because our mother was upset.

Dad remained clueless his entire life as to when the initial treatment with tranquilizers began and how long the initial treatment lasted. Still, he always assumed her struggle began with that first break at age twelve. After Mom and Dad's marriage, the breakdowns continued and grew in severity; consequently, the need for medications to lessen the anxiety increased. Even in those earliest years of marriage another secret was ongoing. Undetected by my father for several months, our mother was clandestinely purchasing drugs illegally and self-medicating.

Due to her pregnancy, the doctor lessened her tranquilizers, but she found a way to buy them. Many clerks in the 1950s worked behind the counter with the pharmacist when the druggist was overrun with orders. They would get the bottle of medication from the shelf, count the number of prescribed tablets or capsules to fill the prescription, place them in the bottle and ask the druggist to sign off. One particular clerk had been stashing three to five tablets of narcotics here and tranquilizers there until he amassed quite a supply. He had earned a roll of extra money selling them to friends and other observed abusers who entered the store. During inventory, he banked on the druggist believing a mistake had been made in a count. It was impossible to prove who made the mistake. However, it is interesting that the druggist did not recognize that almost every missing drug was a mood-altering substance... or perhaps he did.

The clerk overheard the fabricated story my mother used to play on the sympathy of the druggist. Usually the story involved a lost prescription. The clerk stopped her before she left. They established an elaborate system for Mom to purchase the Darvon and tranquilizers from him. I received Darvon and other narcotics, along with the tranquilizers through the umbilical cord. Love of drug over love of child. I will never believe this choice was really understood by my mother. The power of addiction was becoming so strong and she was so predisposed to addiction that she convinced herself that I would be fine. Addiction forces the mind to engage in mental gymnastics. The leaps of faith she practiced were illogical, but to her, sensible.

While paying bills one month Dad noticed an outflow of money with no noted recipient. He questioned our mother, but she denied any knowledge. However, one trip to the bank revealed her withdrawals for "Cash." When he confronted her with the discovery, she eventually confessed.

My mother had already ingested the drugs well into her pregnancy with me. After my birth, the physicians resumed prescribing tranquilizers for her episodes of severe stress and anxiety. This prescription drug use and abuse continued every day of our lives. Jenny and I were never in the presence of our mother when her system was clean. There may have been some drug-free moments in the earliest days following our births, for Dad shared that her mood rarely shifted outside the normal fluctuations most experience in those earliest years of marriage. Still, after discovering her illegal purchases of narcotics and tranquilizers prior to my birth, Dad assumed she was always taking medications.

If she took them while pregnant with their first child, a problem already existed.

Initially the effect of the drugs was positive for she often genuinely suffered from severe anxiety attacks. The tranquilizers helped. Mom's mood remained calm and pleasant. However, she liked the euphoria and calm the medications created. Our home life probably appeared rather common to any observer. However, rather than work toward inner peace, she preferred the easy calm created by medications. At that point she chose a path from which she never veered or returned. In the early years of addiction, the problem is difficult to detect. A person would have to live daily with the addict and catch that person abusing medications. It was the unpredictable behaviors, loss of joy, and sacrifice of relationships over the ensuing years that exposed her drug abuse to those outside our nuclear family.

According to Dad, Mom's hospitalizations were always for "severe depression" or "severe anxiety." These were the only diagnoses my father knew. Perhaps he could not remember the doctor's various psychiatric terms. Yet he rarely forgot anything regarding Mom's health. She was the love of his life, and he was her protector. Mom's drug use was never revealed to Jenny and me, and many close friends and even family members were unaware of the severe problem it was becoming. Our extended family lived in different States and saw us only during our visits there.

There was no mention at all to Mom's doctors regarding what was happening to Jenny and me. The culture of the Deep South still considered drug abuse a moral failure and a condition that should remain secret. The stigma of being a middle-class addict, or living in a suburban home of drug addiction was condemning. Therefore, I doubt anyone aware of Mom's addiction entertained the thought of getting us help. I imagine most would not have even considered Jenny's and my emotional health. I am deeply alarmed that much of this negative stigma still remains. Even more so I remain concerned that small children are frequently excluded from the family therapy sessions, or do not receive therapy especially related to the emotional issues they experience.

Addicts are treated, and older members of the family often participate in therapy sessions. Still, many young children in the formative years of their life are overlooked.

Dad felt a deep, driving need for spiritual and emotional catharsis. That afternoon in his favorite spot he chose to reveal as much of our family story as was possible. He expressed genuine sorrow for not sharing the full story when talking with her doctors, and especially for not being an advocate for his children. Even though Mom probably suffered from an emotional disorder, no one could treat her emotional pain without first treating her severe drug addiction. Any attempt to help her mental illness would be like searching through the thickest fog for a wounded woman intentionally running away. Mom hid in the fog of addiction, and she allowed no one to cut through the dense fog and touch the deeper issues in her life. Dad did not realize at the time that his silence was helping her hide

Drug abuse places the emotionally ill individual beyond the reach of anyone desiring to help. When an individual develops such a strong craving for drugs that she loses all desire to live without them, healing becomes an impossibility. Of course, with God all things are possible. Sadly, for many addicts the transient euphoria and calm become idols. The person's entire life revolves around creating that manufactured calm and acquiring the drugs that make the euphoria possible. By the time Jenny and I reached late childhood and early adolescence, Mom was devoted to this destructive life with no desire to change. She bowed before the altar of euphoria.

When the dosage that once created her euphoria proved no longer sufficient, she increased the dosage. Early in her life of drug use she made the decision for herself as to when she needed to increase her intake. Her increasing tolerance to the drug and her choice to increase the dosage in spite of all dangerous consequences became another destructive cycle in the life of our family. Her ability to function as a wife, mother and friend suffered by degree with every increase. Initially Mom sought calm in order to function effectively; over time she sought the drug to merely function at the most basic level. Jenny and I were attached to the hem of her dress on this progressive journey into the hell of addictive disease. We were powerfully and destructively affected.

One of the noticeable changes in behavior was her inability to deal with stress. The slightest struggle, concerning major and trivial matters created a high degree of anxiety in her. Her demeanor then turned aggressive and angry, and her ability to tolerate the usual stresses associated with parenting suffered terribly. Eventually, Mom was running for her medications just to endure a normal day. In the 1960s The Rolling Stones were singing of our mother in their ode to Valium addiction among housewives and mothers. The song was entitled "Mother's Little Helper." With simple pointed lyrics the song describes mothers abusing Valium just to handle life's normal routines. I sadly observed the line that referred to a Valium pill, "And it helps her on her way, gets her through her busy day." Our mother lived that lyric.

Jenny and I were not emotionally equipped to understand or adjust to our ever-changing mother. We craved the joyful mother we formerly knew. Now, we lived a fragile existence, our course in life determined by the constant fluctuations of her moods. Jenny and I responded to the stress of walking on eggshells by being either hyper or too sedate. We were now swinging from one state of being into another; we were mimicking our mother's life.

While earning my Masters in Marriage and Family Therapy, I read studies that concluded children of dysfunctional parents will act out that dysfunction in their own lives. This is exactly what Jenny and I were doing. If anyone dared look at Jenny and me, they would have seen the dysfunctional mood swings of our mother. I do not believe any child reared in a home of drug addiction escapes unscathed. I also believe that a child's behavior is quite revealing to the concerned observer, especially those who work with children in a professional capacity.

One day I watched Jenny, six years old, exit the house after her chores. She had rolled her jean legs up to her knees and wore a sleeveless top. The most noticeable element in Jenny's appearance was the half clothes pin she held between her fingers. Puzzled I entered the kitchen where Mom sat in pants that came to her knees. She too wore a sleeveless top and was chain smoking cigarettes. After a drink of water I returned to Jenny and saw her place the half clothespin in her mouth, take a deep drag and exhale. She was smoking the clothespin. Jenny, for some reason, was imitating Mom. It was strange that out of all the people to mimic Jenny chose the one person that inflicted the most pain upon her. Was her young psyche attempting to embrace the distant mother through imitation? By "becoming Mom" was Jenny in some bizarre way creating an emotional connection with her? I can only guess.

Jenny and I were windows into the pain occurring inside the house. Outwardly we were often hyped, as though we had ingested pounds of sugar. In reality we were burning nervous energy. On other occasions we sat too quietly, afraid of doing anything that might prove a mistake. A child's mistakes are often forgivable for there was no harmful or disrespectful intent. However, when living with a parent addicted to drugs, mistakes became serious infractions. Mom did eventually share with us why we were often punished for the most benign mistakes: "Y'all get on my nerves!"

"Mama, Why Do You Hate Jenny?"

"Mama, why don't you brag about Jenny like you do me? You talked about her weight in front of people. She was embarrassed. I could tell. You fuss at her all the time for eating too much. You never fuss at me about anything. Mama, it is bothering me to watch you hit Jenny, too. You hit her almost every day. Mama, do you hate her?"

The most painful dynamic to witness in our home was Mom's physical affection for me in contrast to her overt disdain for Jenny. The arms that initially held us became arms of abuse for seven-year-old Jenny. Many addicts choose a child to serve as their scapegoat, imposing and transferring the guilt and pain from their own life upon the child. As a male I did not meet the criteria for the role of scapegoat. In contrast, Jenny was the perfect victim. As a female child with a pleasing personality, joyful disposition and natural ability to draw others to her, she proved prime fodder for our mother's insatiable need to strike out at another female for receiving everything of which Mom may have felt deprived.

Though emotionally distant from Jenny most of her life, in the first year or so Mom maintained a degree of kindness toward her. Our mother had her tender moments. One of the special memories I continue to embrace is the soft spot my mother had for faith. Though never one of great devotion to the church, still a tear could trickle down her face when hearing 'How Great Thou Art." I never heard my mother or father pray, but as a child I assumed they did, especially Mom. Quite frequently people addicted to drugs are religious. It seems as though they believe they hang by a thread over darkness. Faith in God makes the life of addiction more tolerable. It is interesting that my mother only responded to the more *emotional expressions* of faith. Even her religion had to possess a degree of euphoria. Faith had to *feel good.*

Once our mother allowed mood-altering drugs to seize control of her life, with no desire to break free from their hold, her expressions of dislike for Jenny increased in frequency and severity. Full-blown drug abuse makes it difficult, if not impossible to deal with one's life and the life of others; especially those who represent a lifestyle that the addict feels should have been hers. Mom was going to ensure that Jenny never achieved a full and contented life. She diminished any attention Jenny received from anyone, especially Dad. Furthermore, Mom demanded Dad's every minute and ounce of energy to balance the ledger of her own life, sadly at the expense of Jenny's.

Untreated dysfunction always grows more severe with age. As Jenny and I reached late childhood, Mom's self-medicating dosages had attained substantial and disturbing levels. Often after Mom was hospitalized, she left with new medications that were added to the already expanding list of pills she was secretly acquiring on her own. The continual influx of mood-altering medications allowed Mom to amass a considerable *stash*. Large amounts of medications in the house meant she could take any amount desired.

It was in these years, the mid 1960s, that Valium became her drug of choice. Valium was readily prescribed and therefore, easy to obtain. Soon it became the dark power that ran her life and ultimately ours. As her addiction to Valium increased in strength I continued to be the recipient of hugs, pats on the back and other expressions of love. In contrast, as Mom lost herself in Valium and its euphoria, Jenny received vicious verbal and later physical attacks from Mom. I struggled to make sense of the fact that her euphoria could lead her to embrace her son while simultaneously pushing her daughter away. However, if there is one thing I learned about drug addiction from Mom's life, it was this: drug abuse is illogical, and any attempt to make sense of it is an exercise in futility. Together on the porch, Dad revealed that he was mystified over Mom's hatred of Jenny. Hatred is a strong word, a term so unpleasant Dad and I attempted to avoid using it. However, it continued to seep into the conversation. Perhaps we used the word because it is the only term that adequately described the feelings Mom expressed toward Jenny.

As a child I could not understand my mother's obvious disdain for Jenny. I knew it had something to do with Dad. Though Dad and I attempted to arrive at some conclusion that would explain the unending hatred of Mom for Jenny, at best we were guessing. Yet there was one dynamic that proved obvious and noticeable; it was jealousy. She was jealous of Dad's affection toward Jenny, any degree of affection. Why she needed all of his attention remains a mystery, though it was probably rooted in her relationship with her own father. If Dad displayed any degree of affection toward his daughter, Mom was going to lose control of her emotions and make Jenny pay. This reality was certain.

Mom even tested Dad's affection for her over Jenny. She would confront young Jenny with an accusation that was questionable. Mom was banking on her denials, forcing Dad to believe his wife or daughter. If he chose to believe Jenny or downplay the importance of the issue, he received the cold shoulder the remainder of the evening, and all hell broke loose the following day upon Jenny.

Initially, Dad was unaware of the severe consequences of his behavior for Jenny. Soon, however, he realized Mom's rage was steeped in jealousy and could quickly become a vicious expression of rage. Mom's drug addiction kept her beyond the reach of help regarding her jealousy and anger toward Jenny. In the moving novel, *The Shack,* William P. Young accurately described my mother's inability to love Jenny. He writes, "Some parents are too broken to love (their children) well, and others are too broken to barely love them at all." Jenny was barely loved at all. Before any psychiatrist or counselor could help her realize the brokenness and deal with the issues concerning Jenny, Mom had to first clear her head of the drugs. Only then could her disoriented world begin to disintegrate and once again become reality. Healing only occurs in reality, in truth. However, Mom had no desire to stop taking drugs. Consequently she continued to live in disorientation and dysfunction. I own no recollection, neither did my father, of Mom's desire to break free from drug abuse and find healing. Therefore, the irrational rage she expressed toward Jenny never abated.

In the beginning Mom's jealousy expressed itself in emotional distance. In Jenny's third year the jealousy and accompanying anger became verbal. Body language at times communicates as strongly as words. There was a noticeable lack of hugs and other displays of affection toward Jenny. I received verbal affirmation regularly. This contrast in expressed affection began to rear its head publicly as early as our ages of six and four.

As my father sought peace and reconciliation with me and the past we shared, he claimed he noticed "something was very wrong" with the manner in which Mom responded to her new daughter. He recognized Mom's lack of tenderness and natural nurture toward Jenny. However, he admitted living in denial of this upsetting truth until Mom's dislike for Jenny became overt and verbal. Who wants to believe his wife dislikes one of her children?

Her contempt for Jenny and outward doting upon me embarrassed my father; in reality, it infuriated him. Initially, I relished the attention and love from Mom. Few children dislike the love and attention of their mother, especially in the earliest years of childhood. After all, a mother is the most significant person in the life of young children. Yet, as I grew to understand the verbal attacks against Jenny, and witnessed them with growing regularity, Mom's behavior became confusing. Still, I would never articulate what I thought or felt. I was too afraid. If there is any one emotion I remember most vividly from childhood, it was fear.

My mother often could not cook due to her drugged state, or she didn't want to do it. Addictionologists declare that drug abuse, especially with tranquilizers, saps the addict's energy. Therefore, Jenny cooked and cleaned the house. The very fact that Mom chose Jenny rather than me reveals the victimization of Jenny. I was the obvious choice since I was two years older. Soon Jenny was permanently assigned these tasks. Mentally I can still see Jenny's head peeping just above the stove as she attempted to cook the one meal she knew: spaghetti. On many occasions my father came in and took over the duties and cooked something simple. I am certain Jenny shuddered when he relieved her of the chore, for Jenny would pay for his kindness the next day. Also, if the beds were not made and rooms cleaned, she could expect punishment. She was set up to fail.

The cooking, cleaning, and many other responsibilities placed upon Jenny at such a young age provided Mom with plenty of fodder to verbally attack her. No seven-year-old can perform those household tasks without error. One error was all Mom needed to release her illogical searing anger. If an article of white clothing was accidentally mixed with the colored, Jenny was called "stupid," "retarded," or a "screw-up." The same could happen for a bed not properly made. The excuses Mom used to punish Jenny were numerous, and rarely, if ever justified. I find it sad that Jenny knew more about laundry at age seven than most college students first leaving home.

I will never know if Jenny got back at Mom one week, when forced to cook. After all, just how much retribution can a seven-year-old devise? Still, Jenny seemed to relish Mom's refusal to eat one night. For five days in a row Jenny prepared spaghetti, and also opened a can of creamed corn, the other dish she knew how to cook. The two do not complement one another. Mom said little the first four days; after all, she was the one forcing Jenny to cook. Dad was too kind to criticize and ate it. I forced it down silently. However, on the fifth day Mom had enough. She refused to eat and forbid Jenny to cook for the next few days. She was never to cook spaghetti and creamed corn together again.

Later that night Jenny smiled when I questioned Mom's refusal to eat. It then dawned upon me that Jenny just escaped cooking for a few days for all she knew how to cook were spaghetti and creamed corn. Whether the culinary fiasco was accidental or a brilliant means of besting Mom by a seven-year old I will never know. I do know that spaghetti and creamed corn are not among my favorite dishes.

Whereas I struggled to develop an appetite, Jenny nervously ate. Eating was one of the few pleasures she knew in her young life. She was pretty, but Mom did not believe in her beauty and ensured that others look at Jenny critically. Jenny never believed in her own beauty, both inner and outer. She was indoctrinated with the criticism that she was unpleasant to the eye from the time she first understood the meaning of words like "fat" and "ugly."

Perhaps the most painful reminder of the disparaging effect of Mom's verbal criticisms occurred in later years. Jenny refused to be a bridesmaid in my wedding. Gail and I asked Jenny to serve. We were excited to ask her and felt she would be overjoyed.

We were shocked as Jenny refused each time we asked. We pleaded; still, she refused. Jenny offered no reason. She only said, "I don't want to." Later Mom informed us that Jenny considered herself too fat and did not want to wear the bridesmaid dress.

It broke my heart when Dad later revealed that Mom forbid Jenny to be in the wedding. Mom said to Jenny, "You are too fat and you will make the whole wedding look bad!" Of course these words reek with absurdity, and they are ridiculous. However, Jenny believed them. I cannot look at our wedding photos in peace for this reason. Jenny is glaringly absent. Her belief that she was too fat and ugly for my wedding was instilled in her from age four.

Calling children names is as caustic and damaging as a physical beating. If a child is regularly described as useless, stupid, ugly and a failure, she begins to believe these critiques. The names become self-fulfilling prophecies. Jenny and I received severe lashings with such names, opening wounds that bled for years. Jenny was daily criticized for every inadequacy imaginable; thus her self-esteem never stopped bleeding. Though she tried to live above the names and criticisms, Jenny emotionally heard them all the way to her own serious emotional break. I know, for I heard Jenny describe herself in such demeaning terms. At times it was almost like hearing Mom speak again.

The physical abuse began as Jenny neared age seven. Mom's drug intake dramatically increased during these years. The ability to control her anger and feelings of self-loathing had severely diminished. Losing control of the emotions is one of the common symptoms of addictive disease. Once the destructive emotions are loosed, it is difficult for the addict to reign them in. Mom struck Jenny severely with the open hand, not lightly across the bottom as many small children, but across the face and back. Jenny's head would twist side to side as Mom's hands fiercely struck. Jenny covered her head and balled up, causing my mother to swing wildly, as a woman without the slightest concern that she might inflict severe damage.

I observed my mother behaving as though possessed by some dark malevolent power. Sadly, as Jenny learned to fall to the floor to prevent being struck by the arms, my mother responded by kicking, and she kicked harder than she slapped. Jenny was literally kicked like a yard dog by someone with no compassion. Many would never treat an animal with the ferocity of abuse inflicted upon Jenny, nor should they.

Initially, I attempted to intervene. Listening to verbal abuse weighs easier on the developing conscience than witnessing physical attacks. I learned to ignore the names she called Jenny, but I could not avoid Jenny's screams as Mom slapped and kicked her. The physical beatings were always accompanied by an explosive tirade of curses. It is not exaggeration to describe many of these attacks as brutal. No, they were all brutal. The emotional restraints possessed by most of us are eradicated over time in the life of the addict.

I rushed into the fray one afternoon as Jenny received two vicious blows to the face, grabbed Mom's hands and begged her to stop. Without warning her arms swung my way, knocking me to the floor. Since I suffered from the inability to gain weight and height in those early years, I was the size of boys two years younger than I. Therefore, Mom had no difficulty in knocking me aside. The side of my face stung from the blows as though on fire. I walked around the remainder of the day with a hand print burned into my face and bruises on my thigh where I struck the floor. Mom refused my leaving the house until the print vanished. Tragically, the imprints of the hand and bruises were common for Jenny. I lived in terror of trying to stop the attacks, and in the nauseating reality of helplessly having to witness them. All I could do in those years was to plead for Mom to stop. By the time Mom calmed and ceased, great harm was done. Jenny had suffered terribly.

The physical abuse grew more violent over ensuing years. My inability to respond to the abuse of Jenny could be interpreted by some as apathy. However, only I and others in my position know what it is like as a child to freeze in terror. I could not stop the beatings no matter how deeply they disturbed me, nor could I report them to anyone, especially my father. If I revealed my mother's abuse I would receive a beating of my own as soon as Dad was away; worse, my report would also prompt Mom to make Jenny pay.

Mom actually believed she would not verbally or physically attack Jenny if she did not deserve it. "If she was a better child," I frequently overheard Mom say. Drugs can render a person's conscience impotent, or cause it to create a reality in which the punishment is acceptable and deserved. Jenny was a good child; that was reality. In order to inflict the pain Mom unleashed upon Jenny, she had to silence the conscience or convince herself Jenny deserved it. She most often did the latter.

Witnessing these physical abuses greatly disturbed my psyche. I was swallowing utter terror and hopelessness, storing them deeply within my subconscious. They were becoming a part of every fiber and cell of my being. Unknown to me, I was also beginning to boil with rage.

It was not compassion or the realization that these attacks were wrong that eventually stopped them. Mom simply became too dazed and weakened by Valium to swing. Her muscles had atrophied from lying on the couch and doing little house work at all. Soon, all she could muster was a slow, benign swing that inflicted little or no physical damage. Still, the fact that Mom desired to hurt Jenny made its destructive emotional impact upon Jenny's psyche. Jenny was reared knowing her mother wanted to hurt her. I did not experience this mysterious manifestation of cruelty in my own life; I did, however, witness my sister living daily in a dark, violent world.

As severe as these punishments were, I believe the emotional damage inflicted was far worse. The hand prints on the side of her head always vanished; but the critical names and cruel statements hurled at Jenny broke her heart. Jenny never recovered.

Choosing not to physically fight back, she instead tried to buy Mom's love. For holidays and special occasions she would purchase my mother a gift with saved money. She had tried to purchase Mom's love since age five. Jenny saved her money and had Dad drive her to town to purchase Mom a gift. I have few memories of Mom keeping these gifts. On rare occasions my mother would be thankful. I witnessed my mom throwing gift after gift back at Jenny saying, "You don't mean this!" Jenny would burst into tears, and I literally turned ill. Again, I felt helpless. How could a child get a mother to receive a gift when she despised the giver? In later years I learned to purchase one gift *with Jenny*. If Mom chose to reject the gift, it would be "our gift" refused.

One of the most painful memories I have of Mom rejecting Jenny's gift is related to a shiny brass locket she gave Mom on Mother's Day. Jenny was just a small child. The locket was unwrapped by Mom, eyed, and thrown toward Jenny. It struck her in the head. The memory of the locket hurled from my mother's hand and striking Jenny remains so lucid it disturbs me as a man. Spending too much time with this memory makes me ill. I have lived with such memories for years, trying diligently to ignore them. Today those memories scream in my emotional ears with ferocity. I no longer possess the inner strength to lock them away.

Child development specialist Virginia Satir said, "Every word, facial expression, gesture, or action on the part of a parent gives the child some message about self-worth. It is sad that so many parents don't realize what messages they are sending." The messages Jenny received were destructive, and Mom *did realize* their effect. They dehumanized Jenny. That is one of the more destructive effects of drug addiction: it leads the addict to devalue anyone who might serve as a victim for their unresolved issues. It is easier to hurt "something" than "someone."

There were too many verbal and physical attacks upon Jenny for me to record. As a matter of fact, I could not record them if I so desired. What disturbs me most is not the abusive experiences written here, but rather the painful moments I did not record. They remain written in my psyche and still cause me tremendous pain. I can never forget or make satisfactory peace with them. Through all the years Jenny was a delightful child. She was bright, funny and one of the most caring children I knew.

Once when hospitalized with asthma, I was forced to stop selling flower seeds. If the scout sold a certain amount of seeds, he received a new bugle. Jenny walked into my hospital room with Mom, all smiles. She placed the new bugle in my bed. Jenny had sold all my seeds for me. This is only one of many expressions of love and kindness Jenny managed to perform while being severely hurt. In retrospect, I deeply admire Jenny and feel strong regret for failing to recognize just how special she was. Even more, I regret Mom's inability to recognize the beautiful spirit of her daughter.

Chapter 4

The Scales of Justice?

"Mama, Why Do Adults Like Jenny and Dislike Me?"

"Mama, last night Mr. Burns hit me. We were on our way to the grocery store, and Timothy and I were playing around in the back seat. Suddenly he hit me on my arm and told me to shut up. He didn't hit Timothy. Mrs. Susan looked at him like he did something wrong, and everything got real quiet. No one said anything for a long time. When we got back, Timothy and I went straight to his room and tried to play, but everything felt funny. I wanted to call y'all and tell you to come get me, but I didn't know how to ask for the phone. I was afraid. Mama, why do other grownups treat me funny?"

I am certain family and friends struggled as to how they might respond to Mom's cutting criticism of Jenny, especially with Jenny standing there. They experienced even greater distress as she simultaneously praised me. Those who dared challenge Mom's treatment of Jenny were likely to receive an icy glare and a cold reception. Many friends walked out of our life in our elementary school years. Most simply slipped away, unable to observe Mom's overt attacks upon Jenny, while I received love and adulation. Some remained in touch by phone with an occasional visit. Yet, as the years progressed our family lived in growing isolation. We still maintained some friendships, and these were faithful individuals and families who refused to abandon us. Yet the circle of friendship was diminishing.

This mistreatment of Jenny spawned a dislike for me that was intense in some adults. Douglas Horton said, "Abuse a man unjustly and you will make friends for him." Horton's premise certainly proved true for me. Mom's increasing attacks against Jenny allowed some adults to embrace Jenny as much as possible. However, Mom wasn't going to allow Jenny to receive a helpful degree of praise. She had a way of directing the attention away from Jenny and toward me. Her behavior enabled many of those adults to resent me, even though I was not yet eight years of age.

When it comes to harmful behavior toward children, adults are morally upright. People are basically fair and just and will attempt to do the right thing. The probability of talking Mom into choosing treatment for her addiction, or encouraging her to treat Jenny with dignity and love were exercises in futility. The only avenue available for some concerned adults was to lessen the adulation I received. At this point their method of intervention became dysfunctional. How can you help one child by hurting another child? This action became a misguided means by caring people to establish justice in a family ruled by the injustice of drug addiction.

I was very young, and the concept of justice was beyond my understanding. Still, I intuitively sensed attempts by others to level the playing field for Jenny and me. I often felt the cold distance exhibited by many adults toward me, and even suffered from verbal sniping after someone heard enough of the bitter vitriol Mom spewed at Jenny. Consequently, Jenny and I were both receiving negative messages about our sense of self and especially our worth. Jenny was learning from Mom that she was worthless and unlovable; I was learning the same from some adults outside the house.

Years later I realized how angry I've been at those who projected their rage toward me. How did they expect a young boy to respond to a Mother's doting? Did anyone stop and ask what life was like for a child smothered with adulation? In the early years it was welcomed and comforting. However, with age the praise and boasting embarrassed me.

What happens to the psyche of a child observing his sibling and playmate daily suffering abuse? Watching someone you love suffer from harsh, calculated criticism and punishment from the hand of the mother you adore tears at the soul. I was overwhelmed by a strong sense of powerlessness. Furthermore, most friends and especially family members did not realize that my father was emotionally distancing himself from me in my formative years. Many, including my father, felt they could not walk away from the abuse of Jenny without doing something. But what? Diminishing the praise and affirmation I received became the only recourse for some, including my Dad. The more Mom ran Jenny into the ground, the more angelic Jenny appeared to them. The more Mom sat me upon the clouds of heaven, the more sinister I appeared.

It was the mid-1960s, and avenues of intervention and proper responses to children affected by parental drug abuse were unknown. As a nation we had yet to develop a functional means of intervening on behalf of such children. Caring people did the best they could with very few helpful suggestions and limited resources. Sadly, such suggestions and adequate resources still remain beyond the reach of most people, if they exist at all. Some materials and resources may exist, but our culture does not present them in a manner that says, "This is a serious matter!"

My wife Gail is an identical twin. Her sister Nell is very dear to us and a special person in her own right. Her mother shared that when they were children all things had to be equal. If one requested a drink of water, both received a glass. However, their mother would then have to put the same amount of water into each glass. She would add some, pour out some, until with the eye the amounts looked identical. In our home my glass of affirmation was full, too full. Many adults did not know how to fill Jenny's since Mom wasn't going to let anyone do much for her. All they knew to do was empty my glass to make things *appear* more just. At best they established the appearance of justice. In reality they created one emptier glass, and another that for a while looked at least a little fuller. In our home that second glass was always going to be emptied again and the injustice reestablished. Equality for Jenny and me lacked real substance and longevity.

On one occasion the attempt to bring me down a notch or two after hearing enough bitter criticism of Jenny turned violent. Sleeping over at a friend's house was always a great adventure for a young child. While spending the evening with one of my close friends from a family with whom Mom and Dad spent a lot of leisure time, an unforgettable incident occurred. The entire family loaded into the car and journeyed to buy ice cream. Like most excited young boys we played in the back seat and became rather boisterous. The father asked us to keep it down, and we stopped. I leaned forward and propped my arms on the middle of the front seat. My friend gave me a good poke in the ribs and I said, "Stop it." My tone was neither loud nor unusual. It was just a request to stop in order to obey his father. Suddenly I felt a hard blow against my shoulder. His father had taken his right hand off the steering wheel and backhanded my shoulder. The blow, though hard, was glancing and hurt very little. However, I was stunned, and my feelings were deeply hurt. More than anything, I was just confused.

I recall his wife glaring at him as though he had done something to irritate her. Indeed he had; for he had struck the child of another family. Instead of apologizing or offering an explanation, he glared back at his wife and in a harsh tone ordered me to sit back and remain there. I wanted to go home but was afraid to ask. That night we did not play and went to bed early. I remained awake most of the evening, afraid he would enter the room. The next morning he left for work; we played a few hours, and Mom picked me up. I said nothing, for I just wanted to forget it happened. Also, I was embarrassed. I believed the father disliked me. In later years I happened upon his son as a teen who for some reason did not want to forget the incident. He said, "Craig, I hate what Dad did, but it really wasn't about you. I heard him talk to Mom that night when you left. He told her he just didn't like the way your Mom treated Jenny. I don't know what that had to do with his hitting you, but that is what he said." I was thankful for the explanation, but so much for logic.

On another occasion such attempts to belittle me were so absurd as to be humorous. At the time they were not funny; but as I matured the attempts were so outrageous I am able to laugh at them. One afternoon Jenny and I had purchased teddy bears. I bought a blue one and Jenny a red. The bears were identical other than color. Two adult friends visited the family, and their dislike of Mom's inequity in the manner in which she parented Jenny and me was obvious. Their visits became more strained through the years, and like many friends of the family, they slowly disappeared from our life. Jenny and I were proud of our bears and showed them to the couple. Immediately the man said, "I like the red color best." The comment was odd, and a disconcerting quiet settled over the room. His wife responded in a manner to restore peace, "Oh I think they are both nice." He responded, "No, I like the red one!" She responded with an icy glare. Dad then asked Jenny and me to go to our room and play. We listened from down the small hallway. Nothing else was said about the bears and the preferred color. We did notice the wife said little, very little. I imagine a marital argument occurred once they were home.

In later years I considered an adult trying to demean a young boy over the color of a teddy bear as nonsense. However, such strange moments revealed the strong, illogical emotion roused by Mom's mistreatment of Jenny and her doting over me. Rage over injustice is often unreasonable, and the angry person simply wants to strike out against the wrong. On that occasion a blue teddy bear vicariously served as the victim needed to satisfy a grown man's sense of justice.

Perhaps the most difficult aspect in understanding these cold and distant treatments of me was that some believed Mom and I conspired against Jenny. It was as though they thought we sat at the table and devised a means for me to secure all the praise while denying Jenny a single good word. I know it sounds ridiculous. But, that is the point. Addiction tempts people to act ridiculous because the disease itself is so illogical. It makes no sense to yield control of one's life to a drug. It makes no sense to value that drug over everyone and everything. It makes no sense to risk death just to take a medication. Consequently, believing the addict devised a conspiracy with the favored child is not as bizarre as some might think. Even when such a conspiracy is defrocked and exposed as ridiculous, we are left with the illogical: an addicted mother loves and adores her son while hating her daughter. I learned as a child this truth was painfully strange and real, far too real. Our life would only become more confusing in years to come.

"Dad, Mom is Getting Worse!"

"Jenny! Better be quiet. Mama's really sick. Something is wrong with Granddaddy and she is in the back room crying. I saw her for a second, but a woman made me leave. She said me and you could make things worse if we didn't behave. Let's just stay in the den and wait for Daddy." (Dad never came to us that night.)

The catalyst in Mom's downward spiral of addiction was her father's death from pancreatic cancer. I had now entered mid-late childhood with Jenny a couple of years behind. We depended upon two realities to emotionally survive. We needed our Dad. Secondly, we needed for Mom to avoid as much stress as possible. Any event that upset her could result in lifeless depression. Depression becomes a common consequence of prolonged drug use. The user must always come down from the high. This descent always leaves the addict in emotional depths that are difficult to escape. Sadly, the one avenue of escape Mom chose was to achieve as many euphoric experiences as possible. When a painful loss plunges the addict into depression, she can slip into a life of rapid ups and downs. Such an event was about to occur, creating such a strong degree of instability that our home life was permanently altered.

The man from whom Mom craved attention and approval passed away. For six months he suffered at home. There were few available treatments. The family chose not to tell him he was dying. Withholding such information was far more common in those years. The severe consequence from failing to inform a person of their impending death was that they felt no urgent need for resolution of the broken relationships in their life. His death would also leave Dad with the tremendous responsibility of filling her longing for attention and affection from a significant male. From Mom's perspective there was no room for any other woman in Dad's life, especially Jenny.

Our grandfather's death provided Mom with justification to continue her self-medicating. I clearly remember Mom saying, "If I don't take my Valium, I am going to fall apart." As she spoke she held the plastic bottle with shaking hands. Dad did not confront her when she openly took more of the drug. He knew her father's death was devastating, and he feared she might emotionally break with no return.

Mom had by this time totally surrendered her emotional and spiritual strength to Valium. The drug would now do for her what the natural inner coping mechanisms did for others. Those who walk into pain and face it, emerge stronger. Mom never walked into the pain, at least not unless medicated. Mom masked and numbed the pain. She was flying through her difficulties on the wind of addiction. This wind would eventually cease and create a dramatic dive into despair. She would then ingest more of the medication to lessen the effect of the pain. This was the cycle of spiritual, emotional and physical death.

My grandfather's diagnosis proved devastating to Mom. She fell apart. Jenny and I had never witnessed our mother so broken and disconnected from everyone. Within a few hours she was on the bed, holding her knees to her chest. Though Mom was so often abusive and unreasonable, still, she was our mother. We loved her.

While in ministry I attended a seminar on *children of abusive parents*. Someone asked the lecturer, "How can abused children continue to love the abusive parent?"

The answer was enlightening, "Abused children prove the statement true that we can do almost anything when we do not have an alternative. These children still have only two parents. Children naturally love their parents unconditionally, especially in the early years. They love them because they have no alternative. If they hate the parent, what have they gained? Are they more secure?"

Friends of the family were called by Dad the night Mom received Granddaddy's diagnosis. He needed help. He would do anything to keep Mom out of the hospital and sane. When they arrived, Jenny and I were hyper. The stressful energy loosed in the house directly affected us. We walked back and forth to the room where our mother lay in a fetal position on the bed. We were constantly shooed away from the bedroom where our mother suffered. Like boomerangs we returned. We were fearful something very bad was happening to our mama. Children often refuse to leave because they have a strange belief their presence can keep bad things from happening. Eventually we were so strongly admonished, we were afraid to return to the room.

Everyone was so concerned about Mom that Jenny and I were left on our own. Like most children left alone for over an hour, we grew bored. I switched on the television. Suddenly a woman, rarely seen by us, rushed from Mom's side and verbally assaulted Jenny and me. She switched the television off and stormed back into the bedroom snidely saying, "Listen, your mother is in bad shape. Try to act like you care!" Act like we cared? Years later I remembered her words and bristled with anger. She was only one example of how little people outside of our family really knew what was going on under our roof, especially to Jenny and me. We fell asleep on the couch long before anyone noticed that we should be put to bed. Our feelings were totally ignored.

Dad had also called our family doctor. In those days doctors still made house calls. He arrived about ninety minutes after the call. As he entered our small house, Dad welcomed him as though he were royalty and possessed tremendous power. When the doctor knocked on the door, Dad turned to Jenny and me and said sternly, "Be absolutely quiet! The doctor is here!" The next morning Mom was still asleep. Dad remained at home until she fully awakened. His boss was kind and told him to stay with Mom the remainder of the day. He was overjoyed. Though he did not know exactly how he would do it, nevertheless, he was not going to allow our mom to mentally slip away. We heard Dad tell a neighbor that Mom continued to sleep because the doctor had given her a big shot the previous night.

Years later Dad informed me she received a whopping dose of Valium that night. The shot, along with the huge dosage she had taken during the day, placed her into a deep sleep. Dad still had no idea how much Valium she was actually taking. He was in the dark concerning the dosages of her self-medicating. When she awakened that afternoon, most of the friends had left. Dad helped steady her as she stumbled around the house for another hour or so. The shot provided the desired effect. Mom was too numb to feel the pain of the news for several hours. When the effect of the shot began to wane she hit her supply of tablets and took enough to remain numb. Jenny and I kept our distance from her.

Several months after Mom's severe breakdown at home I was called to the principal's office. When a child in elementary school is called to the principal's office, it conjures up terrifying thoughts. What did I do wrong? Am I in trouble? As I walked into the small dingy office, my Dad stood waiting. He said nothing to me, just smiled, but a very restrained smile. After turning to thank the secretary and principal, he walked me to the car. I knew from the silence and serious expression on Dad's face that Granddaddy had died. Though we still had not been told that he would soon die, Jenny and I sensed it, knew it.

Every child usually loses a grandparent. Families mourn, accept the reality of death and the hope of heaven, and then move on in life. However, for our family the death of my grandfather added a powerful stress that pushed my mother into greater depths of depression. Mom never emotionally recovered from his death. Dad became her salvation, I remained "her favored child", and Jenny remained her victim, rival, and bane. Freud defined depression as anger turned inward. The drug addict internalizes that anger severely. However, through the use of medication they can periodically project that anger outside of themselves. While Mom suffered from depression she disconnected herself from life and those in it; yet as she medicinally rose from the depression she turned viciously aggressive toward Jenny.

The death of her father led her to demand so much emotional support that meeting her needs became an impossibility for Dad. Nothing he could do ensured her happiness and emotional stability. Jenny and I felt his stress. We noticed his loss of smile and the diminished time spent with us. He had no choice if he wanted to keep Mom's emotional feet on the ground. The downhill slide into addiction's dark abyss now quickened. As the abyss opened, Jenny and I literally felt that "all hell broke loose."

"Why Do Other People Live Differently Than Us?"

"Jenny, please stop lying. You are just asking for it. I don't understand why you are doing it. Jenny, please stop! You are making Mom act worse!"

Jenny and I were required to live in two worlds of drastic contradiction. Each world had its own language, rules, and discipline. In public Jenny and I used our energy trying to avoid revealing embarrassing information about the secret life at home. Many adults cannot begin to understand the energy required by a child to maintain a family secret. Children by nature are curious, creative, and love to play; however, we expended much of the energy children employ for these delights by guarding our every word. One wrong word resulted in harsh punishment. It was in this arena that Jenny and I were treated most alike. Mom's wrath exploded with equal force upon either of us if we allowed an outsider to know of her use of medicine, or her abusive language and behavior.

Though as small children we were unaware of a condition called "addiction," or the names of medications, we could still say too much. On one occasion I said, "Our mama's been sick. She had to lie on the couch yesterday." The screaming began as soon as I entered the door at home. Still clueless as to why this statement was wrong, I just accepted the truth that we were to say nothing without prior approval. How does a child clear what he "might say" with a parent? Once again the illogical nature of addiction rears its head. A cutting word or vicious physical blow was our teacher.

Jenny always seemed to have a knack for revealing something at home that proved most embarrassing for Mom. Jenny was too young to intentionally attempt to embarrass Mom; actually, she just had a talent for it. Our secret life at home was well-kept, but if there was any window into that life, it was Jenny's actions and behaviors. One night Mom and Dad, along with two other couples, fried fish outside and were drinking beer. Someone asked Mom if she liked beer. Before Mom could answer Jenny responded for her. "My Mom does not like beer, she only drinks it to flush out her kidneys. Her kidneys need flushing a lot." I noticed the couples attempting to stifle their laughter. Mom's face reddened, and I knew Jenny was in for it.

However, that is exactly what Mom told us about her beer drinking. I once asked her why she drank beer. As a curious boy I grabbed an almost empty can, and the taste was bitter. I could not understand why anyone would drink beer over tea or coke. Mom did not want me to get the impression that drinking beer was okay or that she drank it regularly. Therefore, she offered the explanation about her kidneys. It was her fault for believing that kind of explanation would never be repeated, especially with inquisitive Jenny about the house.

For Jenny and me, the two worlds of our childhood were to remain disconnected. Keeping the social and private realms of life separate was no easy task for a child. If life was not already chaotic enough, we lived in swirling confusion. Socially we were growing more disoriented. We knew that some individuals on the outside knew our mother was sick, yet we were still to act as though no one knew. Any time a child is hindered from the process of integrating the outside world with his world at home emotional dysfunction is likely to occur. Though defining "normal" is subjective and open to debate, it is certain that Jenny and I did not live a normal life as children.

Jenny eventually created an alternate world as she entered prepubescence, one that was as dysfunctional as the abusive world in which she lived. This fictional world was created because she could not integrate the two worlds of our life. She fashioned this reality through lying. Jenny would lie when the truth was actually more helpful. For example, Mom asked Jenny about the weather, for Mom often remained on the couch so long she was clueless as to the weather. If Jenny told the truth, "It is not raining, but cold," she would have escaped Mom's sarcasm. Yet, Jenny would say, "It is just a little cool and raining." The lie was obvious and easily exposed. When asked why she lied Jenny offered no answer. This situation drove Mom into a rage and forced Dad into a difficult position. He had to agree with his wife that Jenny was lying and needed discipline; however, he knew Mom's abuse of Jenny was possible. Consequently, he had to walk a careful line in disciplining Jenny and protecting her.

Jenny was manufacturing a world that could inflict pain upon her abusive mother; and she did so in a distorted, illogical manner. She was forcing Mom to deal with a problem her despised daughter created. Jenny had flipped the conflict. In my adult conversations with Jenny, which were too rare, I did recognize that at some point Jenny concluded being a victim earned her nothing but sympathy from others. The sympathy did nothing to change her life or diminish Mom's mistreatment of her. Jenny had discovered a manner of gaining some degree of control over her own life. The world Jenny created with lies was *her world!* No one had the power to take it away. Since Mom was going to abuse her anyway, Jenny was now forcing Mom to deal with a lie and daring her to describe the lie to others as justification for the painful punishments.

As a witness to Jenny's initial breaks from reality, I now realize Jenny was throwing Mom's distorted punitive world back at her. She would fight Mom's distorted view of reality with her own distorted reality. Why was this break with reality inevitable? No person could suffer the abuse Jenny experienced her entire life and feel good about herself. When children are physically and emotionally belittled, their creative energy and energetic spirit are employed trying to survive. Furthermore, Jenny was destined to create her alternate world because she did not possess the ability to integrate what was occurring in our home with the reality outside.

The lying continued for over a year. Our mother convinced Dad that Jenny was sick and needed counseling. Jenny saw a counselor who worked for the state. This was the first and only occasion when Jenny and I saw a professional therapist. He eventually asked to see the entire family together. In stunned amazement I listened to Mom describe the antisocial behaviors of her "dear daughter." Dad simply sat there. His silence was interpreted as agreement. I even took his silence as affirming Mom's accusations. I said nothing as well. Dad informed me prior to entering the car that the doctor would know what I was thinking, no matter what I said. Granting doctors tremendous power, Dad really believed the counselor was a mind reader, and the therapist's observations correct. Therefore, Dad and Mom followed his advice without question.

A shocking consequence occurred from these sessions. Jenny was admitted to a state hospital that housed the criminally insane and those suffering severe cases of mental illness. I was now old enough to know it was Mom who needed to be in the hospital, not Jenny. In later years Dad cried over Jenny's hospitalization. I cried with him.

I vividly remember crying the day we took Jenny to that hospital. Judged an antisocial chronic liar, Jenny was admitted. Our entire family drove her the one hundred fifty miles to the hospital. That drive was the most silent in my life. I particularly observed Mom's behavior. She was totally relaxed, as though out for a Sunday drive. She had ingested several Valium tablets that morning. I know, for I saw her. No wonder she sat so calmly. I maintained the hope that Dad would recognize the injustice of what was occurring, stop and turn the car around. All hope vanished as we pulled into the entrance of the hospital. Jenny? She sat quietly, but nervously fidgeting the entire trip.

We helped Jenny settle into a sparsely furnished room painted a dank color that had become dirty with smudges over the years. We hugged her goodbye and Jenny broke down and cried. I watched Dad hurry from the room with tears in his eyes, saying as he left, "I will be back soon to get you." Mom hugged Jenny. Jenny looked as though she were a piece of stone. Mom's eyes were tearless. For some reason I watched every movement and listened for every word that day. I hate remembering that goodbye even now.

Once in the car I looked back toward the window of Jenny's room; it faced the parking area. I waved at Jenny, and she waved back. It was then that I broke down. I felt a great injustice was occurring, and I could say or do nothing to stop it. Mom used this admission to the state hospital the remainder of Jenny's adolescence to convince those who wanted to support Jenny that her daughter was really a manipulative child. "You can't believe what she says. She was in the state hospital for lying!" I heard that excuse as a reason to disbelieve and dislike Jenny so often it still sickens me to think about it.

Upon her return, the creation of the alternate realities and scenarios continued. These were the only means of escape Jenny had from the constant abuse. As Jenny failed to integrate her two worlds, her personality became compartmentalized and fragmented. Jenny would adopt lying as a means of escaping any painful event or circumstance for the remainder of her life.

Jenny never ceased craving the approval and love of Mom and others; yet she really believed she possessed no lovable qualities. Our mother's rejection possessed far more power than any attempt by Jenny to overcome it. As an adult her attempts to integrate her secret life at home with the world outside reached its crescendo. Jenny suffered from severe bipolar illness. In bipolar illness the normal mood fluctuations severely spike. The mood escalates into a state of giddiness and uncontrollable energy and is quickly followed by a plunge into the depths of depression. These spikes are frequent and severe. I drove to a hospital to pick Jenny up after a hospital stay following an attempted suicide. The doctor called me into a room alone and informed me, "There is no one here with a case of bipolar illness worse than your sister's." Though her mood swings first appeared in late adolescence, it was in her thirties that they began to swing violently from one erratic state to another.

When a child's life revolves around a parent's dysfunction, her self worth will suffer. Dysfunction births dysfunction. Every member of our family lived bound to our mother's addiction and its accompanying behaviors and beliefs. We had a sick mother and were forbidden to talk about it. Jenny and I both left childhood as damaged goods. We concluded early in life that something must be wrong with the entire family. After all, if we were normal, then why did we live so secretly?

Chapter 5

Remedies?

"Why Didn't You Do Something?"

(Together on his porch he had stopped to regain his composure as he spoke of the abuse and Mom's dishonesty in purchasing drugs.) "Dad, didn't you see what she was doing to herself? And, what about what she was doing to Jenny and me? I don't just mean the abuse, I mean the way she used us. I know it had to affect you."

Dad was an enabler. As a matter of fact, he was the perfect enabler. Enablers are almost always loving people who refuse to relinquish hope. Even when hope wears thin, they keep the addict near for fear they might lose them. Dad was such a man. One of the peculiarities that aided my father in his role of enabler was his idolization of doctors. He never questioned their prognosis or diagnosis. Over his lifetime he never sought a second opinion. In the later years of his life he faced a major battle with cancer. The small-town surgeon claimed radical surgery was the best method for treatment. Although his friends and family pleaded with him to receive a second opinion, he refused. He underwent a surgery so radical his family physician was angered.

One of Mom's psychiatrists in the early years of marriage made the statement, "I am afraid without her medication she could end up in an institution, permanently." Other psychiatrists I have met since informed me that Mom was always within reach of being helped. Her condition was never hopeless. The doctor, they claimed, was speaking in exaggerated generalities to let Dad know her depression was serious. However, Dad took the doctor's prognosis to heart and literally. His one driving obsession became keeping his wife at home. Mom played this weakness to the hilt, and frequently. Furthermore, her need for a significant male to help her feel wanted and important meshed well with Dad's fear of losing her.

When Dad confronted her over her purchase of illegal drugs, she claimed that since the doctor removed the usual medication, she was afraid of "going crazy." Therefore, for the sake of the family and her desire to stay well, she claimed to buy the drugs out of fear. Dad believed her. If he challenged her, she might grow hysterical and emotionally break down. I cannot convey how real and potent Dad's fear was. He tolerated the intolerable, engaged in behaviors that in later years shamed him, and neglected forming relationships with friends through the years, all in an attempt to keep Mom safely tucked away at home. Many criticisms can be leveled against my father, but there is one truth no one can contest: he loved my mother and would do anything to keep from losing her.

✗   As a teen I escaped the pain of Mom's addiction by remaining out of the house until the wee hours of the morning, especially on week-ends. One morning, around 2:00 A.M. a group of friends joined me at the local Dairy Queen. We were standing in a circle just jabbering. This was a common practice and sight in my hometown. An intoxicated adult man staggered toward us, supported by a younger man to keep him from falling. "Let's go," the younger male urged him. He refused to budge. The man began to go around the circle and ask each of us where our fathers worked. His words were slurred and he weaved back and forth as though about to fall. Each answered. That very week my Dad took a new job, and I did not yet know the name of the company.

The man lit into me with rage and condemnation. "How dare you not know where your own father works!" The man's face was red with anger, and the younger friend now tried to pull him away. I tried to explain my father's new job but the man was so drunk, he refused to listen.

Finally, the younger man calmed him down. However, I was somewhat of an arrogant teen when confronted by an adult. It helped me hide my real insecurity. I said to the man before parting, "I may not know where my Dad works, but I know where he is. He is where he always is, at home with my mother!" The drunken man wanted to respond, but I could tell the words hit home, and he quietly stumbled away. I remember that experience because I knew my words were true. In that single moment I realized I possessed a depth of pride that my Dad above all was committed to holding our home together. His entire life revolved around Mom. If he could maintain her stability, we all could survive, or so he believed. However, it was strange that so much of what Mom did with us and to us remained beyond his knowing.

He appeared stunned that confessional afternoon when I mentioned that Mom *used* Jenny and me. "What do you mean used y'all?" he asked, puzzled. "Dad don't you know Mom used us as drug mules?" I responded.

"Drug mules?" he was completely lost.

"Jenny and I were Mom's mules."

"When?" he asked.

"In the year just before Penny was born and after."

Though I am not using the phrase *drug mule* in the modern sense, still, as prepubescent children we were used to pick up her drugs and deliver them to her. Mom would always park at the far end of the lot and I would enter the drug store. I was clueless regarding my assignment. As far as I knew, I was picking up the medicine my mother needed. What child would refuse such a request?

The first indication that our mother was not just sick, but suffered from a problem, occurred while I was serving as her mule. I entered the particular drug store often and was treated respectfully. I was now about eleven years of age. The clerk shocked and frightened me as I entered on this occasion. In the past her greetings were rather warm and courteous, though in recent weeks she seemed more distant. Her glare was icy that day, and her words curt and sharp. Embarrassed, I looked around; there were no other customers. She walked to the pharmacist, and a conversation ensued. They spoke in soft voices, so I had no idea regarding the nature of their dialogue. However, their hand gestures were quite telling. The clerk was displeased over something. That was the extent of my knowledge. When she returned, she remained cold and acted as though disgusted when looking at me. As a boy about to enter puberty, this was extremely upsetting. What had I done to make this woman treat me so coldly?

Once the prescription was filled, she took the plastic bottle of Valium and threw it into the paper bag with such force I believed the bottom might have burst. I stuttered, "She wants to charge it today." The clerk reached beneath the counter, snatched an invoice pad from the shelf and wrote harshly on the paper, almost throwing the carbon copy my way. It sounds odd to speak of "writing harshly." However, if such an act were possible, she performed it that day. I refrained from running out of the store once the transaction was complete.

Upon entering the car, Mom immediately reached for the bag. I was now crying. "What's wrong?" she asked not looking me in the eye. She was studying the writing on the bottle, and then its contents. Unaware of time, it seemed forever before she looked at me and took a sincere interest in my pain. When I told her the entire story, I expected her to enter the store and take up for me. Instead she simply said halfheartedly, "I'm sorry." It was then that I realized she was more interested in the contents of the bottle than with what was occurring in my young heart.

At that moment I expressed an emotion I usually kept at bay. I was angry, irate. "I am never picking up medicine again," I stated with fire. Still, she did not reply. The remainder of the drive home occurred in disconcerting silence. Once home I ran to my room and did not come out until dinner. The incident was never mentioned. The next time Mom needed her medication picked up,

I heard her call, "Jenny, come on. We are going to the store." That afternoon Jenny became her new drug mule.

Only children of an addictive parent can fully understand the confusion and insecurity arising from their mother's or father's love of a drug over their own children's welfare. Few behaviors demonstrate the power of addictive drugs than the neglect or abuse of a child to gain the euphoria created by the drug. Every day in America children are placed upon altars of rationalization: "The drugs are not harming them," or "using them to pick up my medicine doesn't bother them," are typical mantras used to create the bizarre rationale for using drugs at the expense of the child. The addict actually convinces herself that these mantras are true, even when the behavior of the child eventually screams, "something is wrong!"

Mom's love of drugs was a silent, destructive menace in our earliest childhood. However, as we matured, so did our powers of perception and observation. Initially, we realized that something was wrong with Mom. However, when we developed the ability to understand that our welfare was secondary to acquiring a medication, we felt embarrassing shame and fierce anger. In response, I isolated myself from peers and felt extremely insecure. Yet, in adolescence I burst out of my insulated cocoon as a teen angry at the world. Jenny responded by losing interest in school.

"Something was wrong with Mom, and something must be wrong with us" became the myth we believed. People in the drug stores were beginning to look at Jenny and me as though we were dirty and guilty of unspeakable behavior. Sadly, this myth helped to determine the course of Jenny's life. I survived, a clergyman speeding through life full of energy, creativity, and rage. Jenny continued to create her world of fallacy in an attempt just to survive.

Chapter 6

Physical Consequences

"Dad, Do You Realize that All Three of Your Children Have Suffered and Continue to Suffer Physically?"

(On the porch with Dad)   "Dad, I know you realize how Mama's addiction hurt Jenny and me. But, have you noticed that all of us, including Penny, have been physically sick? Did the doctors ever mention to you that Mama's use of drugs would affect us physically?"

Early in life Jenny and I developed asthma. My illness was far more severe than Jenny's. Asthma is a lung disease that causes the patient to feel as though he cannot breathe. Prior to puberty I felt as though I was being smothered by my mother's doting and over-protective nature. I was hospitalized almost once a year with the illness. These were the years prior to inhalers carried in the pocket. In the hospital I lived beneath a thick plastic oxygen tent. I gazed at the world through those hazy sheets of plastic breathing higher percentages of oxygen to achieve a normal rate of oxygen in my blood. I could see my mother crying and my Dad appearing worried. During those first admissions and treatments I worried that I was dying.

I am confident today that I suffered from a physiological illness. However, I remain equally certain my body was psychosomatically responding to the turbulent world in our home. I do not know which of these was the cause of my asthma; however, I do know that the psychosomatic dynamic greatly exacerbated the biological causes of the illness. Since Mom could not deal with even the most trivial stresses, our home was always tense. Many might consider such a statement as exaggeration, and cannot conceive of living in constant stress. However, we came as close to a fully stressful existence as possible. Jenny and I lived and breathed this tension. I remain mystified to this day that my father did not suffer a heart attack.

The human body is a miraculously created entity. It is God's masterpiece. It is not only amazingly functional, but has a "self-repair" system in its makeup. If we cut our finger, clotting agents and antibodies that fight infection are immediately released. In a matter of hours new skin will generate, eventually the cut disappears, and we are totally healed. God made the psyche to do the same. When the heart is broken and the soul is in pain, the human spirit will attempt to heal itself. We will seek serenity, search for individuals who have the ability to make us feel better and hopeful; and if we cannot find a source of healing, the psyche will scream, "I am broken! Someone please fix me!"

I believe our lungs physically suffered as we wheezed attempting to take in air, but our emotions also were screaming, "Too much!" Jenny and I were suffocating from the stress filling the house. Our ability to breathe the air of creativity, curiosity, and play was damaged. We were taking in our childhood in shallow, careful breaths. In contrast, we were inhaling the stresses related to Mom's addiction all the way down to our toes.

To train as a counselor you must thoroughly examine your own life. Fellow therapists then reality-check your findings. One of my instructors noted my asthma appeared to possess a strong connection to my mother's "smothering love." I was not free to discover who I was, or to develop a strong sense of self. In those early formative years I was my *mother's son*. She was fashioning me into her image of perfection, and it did not fit. Therefore my body responded by refusing to fully take in this uncomfortable imposed idea of who I should be. The atmosphere in our home, as it related to me, was dense with myth, ripe with contradiction, and sated with overcompensation. Emotionally, breathing was like trying to inhale a deep breath of scorching air on a South Georgia July day.

Jenny's asthma on the other hand was again, less severe. However, her illness seemed to have a "don't forget about me" dynamic. Her struggle to breathe was as real and painful as mine. However, as Jenny realized Mom would always express more concern over me, her asthma disappeared. We both heard Mom say, "Jenny has some asthma, but nothing like Craig's." Our mother always used my asthma to lessen sympathy for Jenny. Both of us were beginning to realize Mom's intent to pit us against one another. Jenny's asthma resurfaced in adulthood during those years when she craved a loving companion who might offer her attention.

It is interesting that at age fifteen my asthma left and never returned. What happened in those early teen years? Dad determined I should get a job. Attending school and working in the hours after class allowed me to be out of the house far more than spending time at home. Mom was now so drugged the doting over me greatly diminished. She still considered me her pride and joy, but I no longer had to stand there and hear it. I could now escape the smothering attention and interact with friends. I began to develop a sense of my own self, and thus breathe freely. Certainly there were biological causes of our asthma. However, it is difficult to believe that Mom's smothering or inattentive behaviors were not directly or indirectly related to our well-being.

Mom's use of drugs while we were in the womb had to have some effect on the development of our lungs. Studies have now proven that when pregnant women take narcotics, tranquilizers and other mood-altering drugs, they give birth to low birth weight children. Furthermore, children born to drug addicts develop breathing difficulties and other developmental problems. If drugs did not cause the asthma, they intensified our suffering.

At birth our lungs were probably not as strong as they should have been.

I suffered from severe lack of weight gain. At birth I was a healthy 8 lb, 11ounce baby. Quickly my growth slowed, and I lagged far behind the normal charted weight and height for my age. My mother and maternal grandparents were convinced I suffered from a serious illness. With the help of money from our grandparents I was taken to several specialists from Montgomery to Atlanta. As a matter of fact, I was among the first children in our area to receive scratches on the back to check for allergies.

By the time I was in the eighth grade, I looked as though I was in the third. My body structure was thin and boney. I was placed on a diet high in calories and protein. However, my body refused to respond. Even when placed on prednisone to control the asthma, I did not gain weight as many do who use the medication. It was as though my entire system were tranquilized. In retrospect, it seemed I was the physical manifestation of Mom's depressive moods. As her emotions refused to respond to the life around her, my body was refusing to respond to common forms of stimuli.

Without venturing into boring details regarding all the medical tests, it is more interesting to note that no definitive diagnosis was made for my inability to gain weight. Allergies did play a role in my asthma, but beyond the connection to asthma the doctors could not establish a cause for my lack of physical growth and weight gain.

It is noteworthy that as I began to get out of the house my health dramatically improved. I quickly gained weight and height. A case can be made for the fact that I was just late in "filling out." Still, why was I late? Why was my system so sluggish and slow to respond to the normal processes of life? As noted, the asthma totally disappeared and never returned. The allergies? They disappeared as well. Since they, too, disappeared over time, my instructors in counseling were convinced my autoimmune system may have suffered the effects of the drugs infused into my body as a fetus.

In contrast, Jenny developed a weight problem. When nervous, Jenny ate. I was Mama's "lovable little boy," and Jenny was Mom's "fat girl" Jenny would struggle with weight her entire life. In her forties Jenny had her stomach stapled in an attempt to lose weight and find love. By age 50 she lost so much weight she looked like a stick. Her face was thin and drawn, making her eyes and teeth appear too large. At Christmas that year Jenny looked little like the Jenny I had known as a child and young adult. If my physical development mirrored Mom's depressive moods, then Jenny served as a picture of Mom's agitated, fidgety, nervous anxiety. Whereas Mom swallowed large amounts of pills to feel calm, Jenny swallowed large amounts of food.

Perhaps the most puzzling facet of our health is related to our spine and its supportive structures. For reasons unknown to the neurosurgeons, Jenny, Penny and I had discs with the consistency of Jell-O. I was the first to experience a ruptured disc. One morning I arose and my neck was so stiff and painful I could not turn my head, nor move it up or down. Tests revealed a disc wasn't herniated; it had ruptured. This means the outer layer of tissue had burst, allowing the more fluid part of the disc to spew out, causing the disc to collapse. Once ruptured, the two vertebrae they supported collapsed, bone upon bone. Nerves leading to various areas of the body were pinched and damaged and excruciating pain resulted from the inflamed tissues and nerves. Bone was fused into the damaged area of the neck to stabilize it. However, six months later a second disc in the neck ruptured.

Ten years later I was rear-ended by a small car. I felt my neck snap and experienced unbearable pain in my neck, down my left arm and into my lower back. Over the next hours the pain radiated down the outside of my left leg so severely and unrelentingly I actually thought death had to feel better. I had never experienced pain of this severity, and it wasn't leaving. Over time, all but two of the discs in my neck were removed and replaced with bone and titanium. Two discs in my lower back then ruptured, and I again received fusions with bone and titanium. My soft discs would later lead to my early retirement due to limited movement and unbearable pain. I could handle some of the loss of movement, but the pain was another matter. It is sad that today I have no recollection of how it feels to be pain free. For over fifteen years I have fought chronic pain from weakened discs. The neurosurgeon claimed my pain would increase through the years. His diagnosis proved true.

As a nurse, Jenny understood suffering more than most and empathized with those most down and out. She was known for performing her job over and above what was needed. Returning patients often asked to see Jenny. While walking down the hall of the hospital, she noticed the fingers on one hand growing numb. The numbness did not disappear. Tests were conducted on her cervical spine. Jenny too had a ruptured disc in her neck, requiring a fusion. She experienced pain in her neck and lower back the remainder of her life.

As Penny neared thirty, she began to feel a stiff sharp pain in her neck. Knowing the family history, her neck was immediately examined. Penny's disc was herniated and near rupture. She had witnessed the agony I experienced through six operations and was determined to avoid surgery. Against the doctor's wishes she refused correction of the damaged disc. She was even required to sign a form releasing the doctor from fault should the disc rupture. "I have warned you," he said.

What are the chances of all three children developing discs so soft they rupture with ease? One of the kind neurosurgeons wanted to perform a specific biopsy on one of my remaining discs. Surgeries take something out of you. I have no means of articulating my experience other than using those words. It feels as though something is removed from your life and never fully returns. I could not emotionally or physically go through any type of procedure. Six invasive surgeries on my back were enough. Therefore, I refused. Later I learned there was little that could be done even if the suspected diagnosis was made.

Like the asthma and body weight issues, I remain convinced the drugs we received through the umbilical cord damaged or weakened the tissues of our spine. The drugs may prove totally unrelated to our suffering. However, for all three of us to suffer the very rare occurrence of discs bulging or rupturing raises serious questions about what happened to us in the womb.

A few years ago I told Gail I felt as though I was sewn and screwed together. Outwardly people cannot recognize any signs of my disability. I even force myself to move as others do; yet I pay a high price of increased pain for doing so. I am certain it has something to do with pride and wanting to live as though all is well. Still, my x-rays reveal a spine held together with metal plates and screws. I said, "Gail, I am piecemeal." My body is as fragmented as our childhood.

My Dad, then in his early sixties, was especially compassionate and concerned for me during the operations and especially when I was left in chronic pain. He attended every surgery and called regularly. He knew me well enough to sense the degree of my pain. We never discussed it, but I think to this day he worried that Mom's drug use had something to do with my condition.

Though having already alluded to the emotional suffering experienced by Jenny and me, there remains another dimension of emotional pain directly related to our physical suffering. Our self-worth greatly suffered from the painful abuses in our childhood; furthermore, the physical illnesses that separated us from other children tremendously added to our belief that we were different and "less than."

The physical illness in early life greatly affected my social development. Whereas Jenny was forbidden social interaction of a positive nature with almost everyone solely because of my mother's dysfunctional behavior, I was forbidden because of asthma. Athletics provides the means for boys to develop a sense of teamwork, camaraderie and self-worth. I was sidelined almost my entire childhood. The doctors forbid that I play any sport which taxed my lungs. Also, my body weight and height made some sports too difficult. Therefore, I felt as though I lived outside looking inward. Something was wrong with me. There it was again, that statement and belief that guided, or rather misguided so much of my development as a child.

I now realized my family life was drastically different from others'; therefore, I was different. By the time I entered adolescence I avoided having friends visit my home. Mom now functioned so unpredictably. I feared having a friend witness a Valium-induced scene. I grew more isolated and developed a noticeable loneliness that concerned my Jr. High School teachers. An appointment was scheduled for my parents to meet with a worried teacher. Mom and Dad revealed nothing, claiming to have "no idea why he's acting that way." The teacher concluded my social withdrawal must then be related to the awkwardness of puberty. For me it was better they believe that shot in the dark than know the truth. I did not want anyone to know the truth, neither did my mother and father. The secret was still intact.

After theology school I became a marathon runner. The goal of finishing a marathon became a consuming passion. I could care less regarding how fast I ran those twenty six plus miles; I just wanted to finish. No one would have guessed that I was driven to finish for very personal reasons. If I finished a marathon, it somehow proved to me that I was not weak, standing on the outside. I would join a select group of people who could push the body past reasonable endurance. That morning it was forty- two degrees, and as I reached the twenty-mile mark, my body wanted to collapse. The years of asthma and yet unknown weakness in my back were punishing me every step I ran. Still I placed one foot in front of the other. I suffered from almost complete hypothermia. I had burned every calorie in my body. When I crossed the finish line, I stopped running and my legs refused to move. I feared collapsing. Gail rushed forward and said, "Craig, you are gray!" A team of medics wrapped me in blankets and started hydration. Thirty minutes later I was hydrated and standing in a hot shower. I stood in the steamy water for almost an hour.

As I slowly dressed, every joint aching, Gail waited outside. When I joined her, she emphatically demanded, "You are never doing that again! I can't watch you do that to your body!" She had nothing about which to worry. My marathon days were over. I had finished. I looked my physically weak, isolated past in the eye and confronted it for 26.2 miles. If only every dynamic of my past could be so tangibly conquered.

Chapter 7

Into the Depths

"Mama, Why Don't You Remember Our Name?"

"Daddy, Mama is acting funny. She is crying all the time. She couldn't even remember our names the other day. What did they do to her?"

A few years following her father's death, Mom lost her only brother. Suffering from severe alcoholism he veered off the road in his truck and was killed. Three days passed before the body was found. Wild dogs by then were ravaging the body. His corpse was so damaged, a sealed coffin was required for the funeral.

Mom was especially close to him. Both sought their father's approval without a clear sense they had it. They had become teammates against the accusation of others that they were somehow deficient. I have no memory of any family member speaking disparagingly of my uncle. Naturally, no one spoke of Mom's condition around Jenny and me. Nevertheless, their self-worth suffered, and they found solace in one another. He was an alcoholic, an addict like Mom. It is interesting that both struggled in their relationship with their father.

71

His death, following her father's, was so disturbing to Mom that even the largest dose of Valium proved insufficient to stop her breakdown. When her brother was killed, Dad tried to keep news about the condition of his body from her. As a matter of fact, the entire family tried to hide this horrendous detail. Yet, Mom asked too many questions and discovered the horrifying truth. She soon was hospitalized again in a psychiatric ward.

Shock treatments were still novel in the more rural areas of the Deep South. For many, they were treatments akin to science fiction. However, one hospital within an hour's drive performed this drastic treatment. A patient had to suffer so severely that she was considered to be beyond the reach of conventional methods of healing. Also, one of the dynamics causing the distress had to be depression caused by painful past memories. Mom's doctor knew little else to try. All medications were failing. She needed help and quickly. Dad hoped the treatments would help her forget the painful memories of childhood, though he admitted still not knowing the content of these memories.

Furthermore, he prayed the shock treatments would help her cope with the sting of her recent losses. He had done all within his power to keep Mom safe and at home. Now he was witnessing his greatest fear actually occurring. The treatments were performed. Penny was just a toddler and Jenny and I were in the first years of adolescence. There was one result not thoroughly considered: Mom lost special memories related to Jenny and me. Our mother was forgetting us.

It was very upsetting to Jenny and me when our mother could not remember our names. I cannot describe the way a child feels when his mother does not seem to recognize him, and forgets his name. The painful memories the treatments hoped to eradicate quickly returned, and her emotional misery was as severe as ever.

When the shock treatments failed, the psychiatrist could only return to using combinations of medications. New medications were added to a recommended dosage of Valium. They were attempting to balance the medications so they would work more effectively. Again, Mom began self-medicating upon release from the doctors, and the recommended dosage of Valium recommended by the doctors was far below what she had ingested for years. The doctor shopping and pharmacy hopping continued. The new medications mixed with Mom's self-medicating dosage of Valium exacerbated her erratic behavior and further weakened her ability to cope with stress of any kind. Me? I stewed in anger that my mother could remember her love of Valium and forget my name.

Everyone must feel some degree of control over his life. Mom used medications as strength, Jenny as victim, Dad as enabler and me as the favored son to manipulate her world. She also had a new instrument to control her world: guilt. Mom especially employed guilt associated with the death of her father and brother. Jenny and I regularly heard "You don't give a damn that your grandfather and uncle died!" Those words were screamed at us so frequently that over time we learned to ignore the accusation. Still, in the beginning it hurt, for we loved our grandfather and uncle. Her accusations that we did not care about the death of these two important people in her life continued into late adolescence.

Though we could often ignore her accusations, there was one Valium-induced tirade that deeply embarrassed me. I remember this incident because it marked a moment when her restraint was so weak she bolted from the secret world and ripped into the adolescent world I was just creating outside of our home. Usually, when outsiders visited, there was little abrasive action or talk. Mom, on occasion, still possessed the capability of mustering enough control to pretend all was well. On this particular day she experienced such a loss of self-control that when I prepared to leave with a friend, she grew extremely agitated. Jenny was away, and Mom had planned to pick up a prescription of Valium. She planned to ask me to stop by the drugstore while out and pick up the medication. This was a favor she had not asked in years.

However, I was now old enough to know what she requested. Also, I vividly remembered entering the drugstore for that purpose as a boy, and the treatment I received from the abrasive clerk. I vowed never to place myself in that position again. I walked out the door with the friend, refusing to go to the pharmacy. I did not offer an explanation to her in front of my friend. Keeping her addiction secret was still an important requirement for Jenny and me. Still, Mom screamed as I walked outside toward the car, "You don't care that my brother lay dead for three days! You don't care that he was buried in a sealed coffin!" The tirade continued as the two of us made our way to the car, with Mom now adding the nauseating details about her brother's ravaged body. The entire incident was bizarre. My friend felt my discomfort and embarrassment and felt it himself. He looked at me and simply said, "I am sorry, man."

"It's okay. You couldn't understand, believe me," I softly responded. I don't think anyone could understand such an outburst unless he lived his entire life in an environment of drug addiction and its destructive, erratic behaviors. This moment was also pivotal, for I realized her addiction and erratic behaviors were never going to end. I was immersed in hopelessness and felt very sad. I still loved my Mom and now it was evident I was losing her, really losing her.

"Daddy, Why Don't You Pay Attention to Me?"

*"Daddy, I made the high school baseball team!" "That's good,"
he responded flatly. "It was tough but I made it!" "Good," again
emotionless.*

*"Daddy, why aren't you happy for me? You were a minor
league player and I am doing something you did! Aren't you proud
of me? Daddy, why are you walking out of the room?"*

Jenny and Mom's relationship was contentious and one of the few predictable dynamics in our home. In contrast, my relationship with Dad was unpredictable. Though I knew he loved me, he struggled to display affection and express praise. In fairness, he rarely, if ever, heard praise in his childhood home. I really believe he did not know how to praise his son. My entire childhood was spent admiring and idolizing a father who was our stability, and yet seemed emotionally distant.

If one placed a title on our relationship it would read, "The Father Standing Along the Fence." The game of baseball best defined the father/son bond we shared in childhood and early adolescence. Dad was a minor league baseball player, and a good one. Most boys assumed that my Dad would take an immense interest in teaching me the game. He wasn't interested, or if he was, I didn't know it.

Often a shared sport provides fathers and sons with a conduit for an emotional connection. However, my memories are of Dad standing along the outfield fence, watching me from a distance. He never stood close enough to even talk with me, advise me or encourage me. There was little personal involvement, but he was there. He did coach me one year; other than that, he just watched and said little. There were no childhood games of catch, or lessons in the fundamentals of the game. If there were, they were so infrequent I can't remember a single occasion.

As I played in older baseball leagues, including high school baseball, Dad grew more distant. Making the school team was difficult in my high school. The town boasted of some great professional prospects. Therefore, if a junior made the team it was a major accomplishment. When I read my name on the "made it list," I hurried home to tell him. Mom was proud and I appreciated it, but I wanted Dad to be proud of me. The only words he said to me were, "That's good." He then walked to the kitchen to help Jenny. To be considered a "chip off the old block" would prove to be the ultimate accomplishment for me as a young man. I didn't believe at the time that he cared about having such a son.

As a caring father, he was not immune from feeling anger over the verbal injustice he daily witnessed. Like others, he too valued justice and was upset when Mom lavished affection upon me and belittled Jenny. Yet, how was he to balance the scales when the issue of justice involved his son and daughter? Furthermore, toward whom could he express and articulate his anger? He could only suppress his irritation and rage for so long.

Dad had to provide some sense of justice, even if he could not do it well. Mom had become bitterly condescending of Jenny, with no praise or affection of any kind expressed toward her. One arm on the scales of justice was missing; thus, the sense of household justice was way out of sync. Dad lavished love and affection upon Jenny in the early years to offset Mom's obvious preference for me. Employing my previous metaphor, he was attempting to ensure both glasses were full. Soon, however, he learned that praising Jenny only increased Mom's anger toward her. In response, Dad turned emotionally cold toward me. Addiction affects everyone in the home. That confessional afternoon in the later years of his life helped me realize that the only way he knew to even things out was to do as others: bring me down a notch or two.

Baseball was Dad's ticket out of the effects of the depression in rural Mississippi. However, he had few parenting skills to take with him. When large rural families are trying to survive, the last thing many of them are concerned about is praise. "You do what you have to do," was the mantra by which they lived, escaped, and became productive individuals.

I owe much to one of Dad's sisters and her husband. Growing up without an abundance of praise, she was determined to live a moral life, marry a good, hardworking husband who valued her in turn, and raise a family with praise and touching expressions of care. When my own family seemed to be falling apart, I thought of my Aunt Joyce and Uncle Fred and what they accomplished. They were a ray of hope from Dad's past, and later would help me understand my father far more than I could alone. When children struggle to emotionally survive, they will look for life and light. They will look for expressions of normality. Such light helps the child believe that painful experiences do not have to be acceptable, and something better can exist for them. These were the few sources of hope belonging to Jenny and me. We had to believe a different kind of family life existed and was even possible. If other members of our extended family lived in love and a normal degree of serenity, then perhaps we had a shot. Jenny and I lived in a secret world, and in many ways a dark world; however, there were rays of light breaking through now and then. I never forgot them and owe much of my path out of the pain to those families that remained in our life and modeled a family life that inspired us. Probably unknown to them, they were God's instruments of hope. Uncle Fred and Aunt Joyce's home remains one of the places from the past I visit for nostalgic reasons. They represented what I wanted for my own family one day, and it is good to visit them today and discover my faith in them was not misplaced.

It was the beatings as a young boy that I struggled most to process. My father was a gentle soul and slow to anger. However, when he was angry, he was explosive. Like any child, I misbehaved and deserved discipline. Then, there were occasions when Mom complained about me. They were rare, but always serious. It was a big issue to her when I was not acting like her chosen, preferred son. She almost always used the "wait until your father gets home" manner of discipline with me. Dad's response was to beat me with his open hand, much as Mom struck Jenny. Dad was physically strong, and once his anger was unleashed he struggled to reign it back in. There were many blows, each one harder than the first.

Together on his porch he wept profusely while apologizing. "I know I beat you when you did nothing. Your mother often made no sense. I was just trying to keep her happy." I wept as well and took baby steps toward healing. He, however, took giant leaps with his honest admissions and earnest desire to make all things right.

Our relationship first began to thaw some when I was fifteen. Dad called me into the den as I neared my sixteenth birthday. "You will need to work now. I can always provide a roof over your head and food on the table. But you are going to have to help from now on." I didn't mind the request. He didn't realize how desperately I wanted to get out of that house. I earned my first check at fifteen and have been working ever since. For some reason Dad could talk more easily to another working man than he could to a son. He began to ask me about my job, how much I got paid, and what I planned to do when I graduated from high school. I relished these conversations.

However, he remained a confusing person in my life until his mid to late sixties. He was deprived of an education, so I considered getting an education to be a high priority that he shared. Instead, he fervently tried to convince me to forgo college and work instead. College cost money, and he would rather I pay my way through life from high school graduation onward. Even when amassing enough scholarship money so that he would pay nothing for my education, he still disliked my attending college. I would eventually earn a degree, two masters and a doctorate. He said very little until I earned the doctorate. By that time in life he was unafraid to say "I'm proud of you." Also, he no longer had to balance the scales of justice in a combustible home.

As a young adult I realized that Dad was not intentionally trying to deny my existence in my teen years. By that time Mom's drug abuse had grown so severe it dominated his every waking moment. The cold distance and explosive anger were related to his own feelings of helplessness. He was watching his wife's mind disappear by the month, learning of his daughter's physical abuse while his son was placed on a pedestal, and trying to keep enough money in the bank to feed us all at once. Handling these tasks inflicted a tremendous amount of stress upon him. He needed an outlet. I was a convenient vent for his anger, and at times he used it. It couldn't be Jenny. Jenny was already near breaking. It could never be Penny, my kid sister, for she was just a preschooler. I was the only candidate.

Again, no one lives with an addicted person in the house without being changed and challenged. It will challenge every ounce of tolerance one possesses, challenge everything believed about the addict, and challenge the possibility of reaching every dream in one's heart. We were all trying to survive, and my father was doing the same. In those years he was my father. He was the one stable reality in our home. In later years he became my daddy and my best friend. Drug addiction stole many precious years from us and hindered our relationship as father and son more than most can imagine. I remain unable to articulate what the loss of those years with my father meant to me. I so enjoyed him over the last fifteen years of his life. I could only have become a better man if Dad had not invested so much time, money and energy trying to keep my addicted mother at home. Perhaps he would have taken me under his wing and taught me to play the game I dearly loved. I will never know. Drug addiction had created a painful sense of regret and another question of "what if?"

One day in his middle to late sixties I helped him clean out his attic. He was moving into another house. We found a scrapbook my mother created of his baseball exploits. That afternoon only the two of us were working in the little house. We took a break, and I picked up the scrapbook. Since he never mentioned baseball, I did not ask him any questions. However, he walked over and sat down. Together we looked at the clippings, and for the first time he began to tell me his stories. Although a grown man with children, I felt like a little boy listening with fascination to his father's grand exploits.

After replacing the book and returning to work, I began to realize for the first time what he sacrificed to take care of my mother. Dad was chosen by the Cardinals as a possible player for the Majors. He was a tremendous power hitter and hit for a high average. They pleaded with him to travel to pre-Castro Cuba to play winter ball, but he refused. They asked him to move from the outfield to catcher since they needed catchers in the pros. Again, he refused. Finally, they asked him to play AAA ball to prepare him to move up to the Major League Cardinals. He refused. Why? There was a smiling, beautiful, active woman that he loved, and nothing was going to separate them, not even his career. He lived his entire life ensuring no one took my mother away. He did not realize that Valium had already done that.

"Dad, We Just Had to Get Out of That House!"

(I had gained some control of the conversation with my Dad, for I had explanations of my own that I owed my father. Also, we were trying to understand what happened to Jenny when Mom grew

much weaker physically and emotionally). "Dad, Mama was no longer able to care for us. She spent so many hours sleeping on the couch. I thank God you wanted me to work, because it got me out. But Dad, Jenny never got out, not even when she was physically out. Mentally she was trapped in the house with Mama."

By age seventeen I discovered a means to escape from home and create a new life. In high school I developed the mask of a clown. I was a crazy guy who loved laughs and cared less about grades. My mask made me lots of friends. However, the mask was only another element in my life standing in stark contrast to life at home. I solved that problem by rarely going home. I attended school, worked in the afternoon, and had a good time with my friends every weekend. I only went home in the wee hours of the morning to sleep.

My home life was secret to most in the community, especially my teachers. I studied under perhaps one of the best high school English teachers in the State. He assumed I did not care because I rarely applied myself. One day prior to the bell signaling the beginning of class a friend and I were discussing possible colleges. I revealed that I would love to attend a college several miles from home. My teacher interrupted me and in a condescending tone said, "What is it, Mr. Rikard? You can't wait to leave home?" I did not answer. He did not realize the truth of his words.

Most terrifying in retrospect was my flirtation with death. Of course most teens believe in their invulnerability. However, my dance with death was far more than one of the common characteristics of youth; I seemed determined to look the real possibility directly in the eye. One evening on Hwy. 280 a group of friends and I traveled home following a high school basketball game. "Hey," the driver of the Camero yelled over the music. "Let's see how many cars we can pass without pulling back in!" No one spoke.

"Yea, let's do it," I agreed. Still no answer from the others. The driver pulled into the passing lane and began passing a long line of cars returning from the game and counting them as we passed. One, two, three ... seven." As we passed the seventh car he hesitated and wanted to pull in.

"No!" I yelled. "Keep going."

"No, let's don't," a boy in the back said in alarm.

"Come on," I egged the driver on. "Let's set a record. Don't be chicken." High school boys can bear many names, but chicken is a most bitter name. He pressed the gas pedal to the floor. I watched the speedometer disappear. We passed fifteen cars before pulling back in at over 120 miles an hour. I was elated and thrilled. Adrenalin rushed through my body. I had no idea how close I had come to death. One blown tire, a second of losing control, one car that could not see us, and we would have been killed. Was I trying to feel a part of life by defying death? Did I feel that disconnected from life? I will never know. As I contemplate my behaviors in those years, they frighten me. Thankfully, I escaped those years physically unscathed.

Dad had now started to mellow and was beginning to warm up to me. We began to converse more than ever, though the talk was about practical matters. Riding to work together every day allowed us to talk outside the home. Though praise was still withheld, I began to believe that deep within his heart he was proud of me. I was working and earning my own way. He admired that and always affirmed me for working. In other words, I wasn't yet praised for who I was, but for what I did. At the time, that was sufficient for me. It represented a thaw in the ice.

He became concerned that I was burning the candle at both ends and requested that I come home and sleep more. He feared I could become ill. Poor Dad did not realize that being at home was making me sicker in ways a lack of sleep never could. If I wasn't home, I did not see Jenny's pain, nor did I hear the cruel words and names. These were the sounds and events that lived and breathed in our house, and I was sick of inhaling them.

Though Dad requested I take better care of myself, he never demanded it. It was my choice. This was another peculiar characteristic of Dad that other fathers I knew did not practice. Dad determined that if I earned my own way, my choices were pretty much my own. The only time he expressed concern over one of my decisions was when it threatened my ability to work.

However, the most meaningful means of escape was made possible when I discovered the girl who would become the love of my life. I was deeply attracted to her, not just because of her beauty, but also because she accepted me as I was. She took me without the mask. Many relationships of depth are formed through mutual vulnerability. I slowly revealed bits and pieces of the home life that caused so much hell in my life. Gail shared her own joys and pains from her childhood. Few couples reach a level of intimacy that opens the door to pain, saying, "Here, look! This too is a part of who I am!"

At age nineteen we were mentally older than our age. The two of us had seen and felt so much of life; really, we experienced more than we desired. We never truly had a normal adolescence. We had seen and heard too much. We had both battled self-esteem issues. Our love was authentic. We would marry when I was nineteen, and she was eighteen. Some could say we grew up together. I had started college and was determined to finish. Gail did not love academics, but loved raising children and later was obviously called to be a minister's spouse. It is a special calling in its own right, and no one did it more passionately and gracefully.

We moved away so I could attend college and work. For the first time I felt a true sense of worth. Furthermore, for the first time I considered myself truly emancipated from my former life. My life was now my own, and I had found someone with whom I could meaningfully share it.

Jenny's move out of the house was far more painful. Life at home had become so painful Jenny could not study in peace and did not attend high school. Mom had totally isolated her from every friend and peer. Therefore, Jenny took the GED and enrolled in nursing school in a local technical school. Fortunately for Jenny, the school was out of town. At last there was some freedom. However, Jenny lived with chains wrapped so strongly around her heart, she would never know full freedom. The destructive messages were as much a part of the baggage Jenny took to school as the literal suitcases.

Jenny was so starved for love, and had worn the mask of being a "people pleaser" so long, she became pregnant her first year in school. She never had a date in high school. I later learned Mom had told her no one would dare want to date her looking as she did. Also, Jenny was never around anyone long enough to establish a relationship. Jenny went to high school, then straight home and worked until bedtime. There was no graduation walk or celebration. When Jenny acquired her GED it was as if she had received a common letter in the mail. It was greeted with a yawn. Consequently, the first male that displayed affection and made Jenny feel special stole her heart and took advantage of her vulnerable emotions. After impregnating her, he disappeared.

Gail and I arrived home for a visit, not knowing of Jenny's pregnancy. Mom was sitting outside on the front porch with Dad. As I walked up the steps to greet them, Mom, without a greeting, said, "Your sister's inside. She's gone and got herself pregnant." Her face took on the look of disgust. As I moved quickly inside, Dad ran to accompany me. He really thought his son was going to verbally assault Jenny for making such a mistake. I had recently become a Christian. At the time Dad did not attend church, and from what he had heard, church people thought very badly of girls like Jenny. He was afraid I would do the same. He was going with me to protect her. He was shocked when I grabbed Jenny and hugged her. She cried as we hugged for several minutes, and Dad moved out of the room, relieved. He realized then, that over the years someone else in the house really cared about Jenny.

Jenny did escape the pain of home as a result of the pregnancy. Mom was in no condition to help raise a baby, nor did anyone believe she desired to help Jenny do so. Her suggestion was to send Jenny to a home for unwed mothers, which was followed. It seemed that the only periods of peace from Mom occurred when Jenny entered an institution. She now lived in a home with girls sharing the same fear and uncertain future as she did. Thankfully, Jenny found a degree of solace and care in that home with people she had never known.

Though moving to tech school did not provide an answer for Jenny's shredded self-esteem, still the beautiful person Jenny had always been revealed itself her first Thanksgiving away. She called home and asked to speak to Dad. He took the receiver and listened, waiting for a problem to be articulated. "Daddy, there is a boy here that has no family. He grew up in a boys' home in Ohio. I found him making a bed in the stairwell because the school was closing the dorm. Daddy, he can't spend Thanksgiving sleeping in a stairwell!"

"Bring him home Jenny," Dad replied. He turned to tell Mom we would have a guest for Thanksgiving. These were the years when her drug dosage was so large she began to become disconnected from reality. She walked through life as though in a daze, barely managing to perform the basic tasks. Although there were still occasions when she seemed to awaken to life, they were lessening. She did not walk through the house like a zombie. She just felt no connection with what was happening. The disconnect was an emotional estrangement. She was functioning as a person, but not feeling.

Danny came home with Jenny and ended up living with us for two years. Dad also felt bad for him and tried to provide a home. Jenny's compassion had provided a home for a boy in the stairwell. Out of kindness and necessity Danny helped Mom and my kid sister Penny. Danny and Penny became good friends as he became a big brother to her. I was away at school and Mom could not provide all Penny needed in terms of play and sometimes transportation. Danny was a good big brother and help to Mom. If she was jealous of Mom's kindness toward Danny, Jenny never revealed the slightest evidence of it. If anything she was truly happy that Danny had a home, even if was in the home of her pain.

Chapter 8

The End of Addiction?

"Dad, in Spite of All the Pain Mom Caused, When Mama Died It Hurt Didn't It? I Know It Hurt Me"

"Craig, it hurt when your mama died. I knew good things about her y'all couldn't see because of the drugs. I loved her and I was never lonelier than after her death. Thank God Penny was still at home. But, Jenny still isn't acting right, even with your Mama's death."

Jenny was eight months pregnant and Gail and I were living two hours away in college when the phone rang in the wee hours of the morning. It was Dad. He was crying, and his words were difficult to understand. I was extremely upset. I had rarely heard my Dad cry so severely.

"The doctor said he would not give a nickel for your mother's life."

"Dad, what do you mean? What's wrong?" I asked frantically.

"Your mother is almost dead with pneumonia," he muttered through the tears.

Immediately we packed very few items and raced toward the hospital, over two hours away. I was so terrified I stopped every thirty minutes or so to check in with Dad by phone. Nothing had changed. Dad decided it was best not to tell Jenny since it could endanger the baby. Dad and I both were sure that in light of all that had happened through the years, Jenny was going to react strongly. In spite of the animosity and rage in Jenny's life, she still craved Mom's love more than anything in life. Upon arriving at the hospital Dad was an emotional wreck. The one thing he feared, fought against all of his life, was happening; he was losing the love of his life, addicted or sober.

Gail and I raced to my hometown and joined Dad in the hallway of the hospital. He hugged both of us more tightly than I remembered in my entire life. My hands trembled as we waited for the next doctor's report. Time seemed to move like the old clocks in primary school at 2:30. It took forever for 3:00 to arrive and announce that school was out. I had watched those clocks move one slow tick at a time. Thirty minutes was a lifetime. I was now back in my childhood waiting for time to speed up. At last the doctor appeared and offered news as hopeless as his original diagnosis. However, now he wanted to transfer her to a major hospital forty-five miles away.

Before leaving, Penny was placed with family friends, not knowing what was happening. She was only eight years old. The family was blind to the fact that though she did not understand what was happening, she felt it. I, more than anyone, should have realized what Penny must have felt. The hospital was in the town where Jenny and I spent our childhood. It was the town of dishonest clerks in drug stores, and the origin of the full-blown Valium habit. Now Mom was returning to die.

Dad and I agreed it was time to contact Jenny. As upsetting as the news might be, she needed to know her mom was dying. She deserved the opportunity to deal with her emotions related to the woman she needed to love her most. I wanted to call her and waited until just past 8 A.M. to call. "Jenny," my voice trembled. She intuitively knew something was wrong, severely wrong.

"What is it Craig?" alarm in her voice.

"Mom is near death and they don't give her any hope," I managed to say. "We are in the Palm Park Hospital." I broke down on the phone, and it upset Jenny.

"I need to come," she said urgently after I regained some semblance of composure.

"You can't Jenny," I pleaded "You are ready to deliver. I promise to call you every time we hear something new. Anyway, you couldn't talk with her. She has a breathing tube inserted and is out of it right now."

I said goodbye and prepared to hang up when Jenny stopped me. Now her voice shook with such emotion it scared me. "Tell her I love her." When I placed the phone on the receiver I shook my head over her statement. No one knows, until this writing, that I had to quickly make my way to the small chapel and, once again, release the tears. I mention the tears of Dad and me a lot. It is for good reason. We did not easily cry in adulthood. Only the most moving and terrifying events could lead us to break. Jenny's words revealed the true power of love and just how much we need it. That striking reality broke me. Later I would wonder at the power of love to overlook the worst in a parent.

Jenny gave birth a few days later. She had a son, Chris. A family friend and I planned to drive to the city and bring Jenny and her new son home. We had hopes of Jenny seeing Mom before she passed. Jenny and the new baby were taken to our family home to settle in; I would drive her to the hospital as soon as all was arranged for care of her new son. Mom died before Jenny could see her. I was also away from the hospital when she died.

However, my last visit was most memorable. I will cling to that memory the remainder of my life, especially when the painful memories rear their head. Mom had a respirator tube placed in her trachea and could not talk during the entire illness. She wrote on a pad until she was too weak. Then, she made small hand gestures. When I entered her ICU cubicle, she pointed at me. I spoke the words I thought she attempted to say. She nodded in the affirmative when I got the word right.

"Me?" She nodded and placed her hands in the posture a little child would use when saying grace at the table; her hands folded in a position of prayer.

"Prayer? You want me to pray?" I asked. She managed to shake her head vigorously. She then pointed to her chest.

"You want me to pray for you?" Now she nodded, and tears trickled from her eyes. I prayed aloud that Christ would enter her heart and grant her peace. I was a new Christian and offered a simple prayer for the two things I had most wanted over the years. I wanted her to have a change of heart, and peace instead of the chaos and rage that had made our lives, including hers, so miserable. She mouthed "Thank you." It was my last conversation with my mother. She died only hours later at the young age of forty six. I believe for the first time in my life, my mother was clean. Death accomplished what life and all its wonders never could. I had hope that at last my mother looked at me with clear eyes.

As the hours following her death passed, I began to feel an overwhelming sense of ambivalence. So much about her life angered me. Oddly, I never realized just how angry I was until she passed. On the other hand, I realized I loved her, and loved her deeply. In later years I would wrestle with the psychological truth that anger and love could coexist. I deeply mourned. Gail joined me with her own tears. She knew I hurt and was aware of the reasons behind my deep pain. Gail did not understand the depth of the abuse in which Jenny and I had lived. However, she knew enough to feel great pity for Jenny.

Mom's refusal to let Jenny participate in our wedding deeply hurt her. Gail's mother was a very saintly woman and never would have treated someone in that manner. Mom's behavior was difficult for Gail to understand. However, in the last couple of years Mom revealed greater depths of her dysfunctional behavior toward Jenny. Mom took the jewelry Jenny owned and gave it to Gail. It wasn't Mom's to give. Gail was stunned. Mom said to her, "Here, you keep these. Jenny never takes care of anything anyway." Naturally, the gifts were not kept. However,

Mom's cold manner in giving Jenny's personal possessions away deeply bothered Gail.

Still, when Mom died Jenny wept profusely. I knew so much of Jenny's tears were related to a relationship never reconciled. She and our mother were at odds her entire life and Mon died without asking to see Jenny. She did ask about the baby. I used that request to make Jenny believe our mother was interested in her. The relationship died as it lived, broken and full of regret.

Jenny and I awaited the arrival of Dad from the hospital. When he walked through the door, Penny was the first to speak. She had never seen her father weep as he did. He was totally broken. Penny spoke in her young voice, "Mama's dead isn't she? I know she is!" and she began to cry while clinging to Dad. Penny's young words reveal that children know more than we think. She intuitively felt Mom's death. She read the faces entering the door and felt the unexpressed.

Unknown to everyone but Dad, Penny had experienced Mom's growing dysfunction from drugs two years prior to Mom's death. Dad was driving Mom and Penny to Memphis to visit his family members. Stopping in a small Alabama town to stretch, Mom entered a small department store. She picked up a cheap scarf and stuffed it in her purse, then walked out the door. Mom could have purchased the scarf twenty times over. Why she stole the scarf Dad never knew. The business caught her, and with Penny standing beside her she was arrested. It took Dad hours to clear up the mess as Penny was experiencing terror. Only about five years of age, Penny did not know if she, herself was bound for jail along with her mother. The moment was traumatic. Most striking was the calm Mom maintained during the entire experience. She was so drugged, she was living in another reality; it was a world where stealing cheap scarves made sense, even if it terrified your child. The police called Mom's psychiatrist and after a brief discussion released Mom with no charges. The doctor informed the police chief that Mom was "a very sick woman." Who knows the range of emotions Penny felt when Mom died?

Gail and I also broke down further when Dad entered sobbing. "She's gone!" he cried. The woman he loved and protected at all cost was taken by an illness over which he had no control. He was right; she was gone. But, for Jenny especially, she was never gone.

Over the ensuing five years Jenny visited Mom's grave more than anyone. Dad visited for several months, but finally shared with me that it hurt too badly to visit. He simply tried to ensure flowers were placed on the grave. Jenny usually handled that for him. I believe even in death Jenny was reaching for some sense of serenity related to her mother. Mom refused Jenny's gifts as a cruel act of displeasure. Now she could not refuse the visits or the flowers her daughter placed on her grave.

"Daddy, Why Is There So Much Valium in the House?"

(Mom had passed away the prior week) *"Dad, we need to begin to clean out some closets and drawers if you are ready."*

"Yeah, I believe it's time to start," he almost whispered.

I walked into the den about an hour later and in stunned amazement said, "God, Dad! There is Valium everywhere! I am finding bottles in drawers, the tops of closets and even hidden away in the strangest places." He was not stunned at all.

In later life it hurt us to remember who our mother might have been without the large dosage of drugs. That is one of more painful realities a child of an addict experiences. We feel as though our parent was stolen from us. The ransom to get her back was a detox and treatment program. Mom would never pay that price, and Dad was afraid to push her too forcefully. Therefore, our mother was on drugs every hour of our time together.

Most recovering addicts will tell you they had a drug of choice; it was pointedly obvious that my mother loved Valium. She complained mostly of anxiety and depression, both treatable with Valium. Using her past admissions to psychiatric units as fodder to convince the doctor of her genuine illness, obtaining a prescription was not difficult. There were also orthopedic physicians to whom she complained of severe back spasms, another condition Valium helped. After many tests on her spine, no specific diagnosis could be made. Still, there were a few doctors who prescribed Valium for the spasms, and sometimes narcotics for the pain.

The insurance companies had not yet developed a computerized means of handling pharmacy claims. However, so as not to arouse suspicion, Mom only filed two to three of the prescriptions on insurance; and she filed the claims a couple of weeks apart. She continued to pay cash for the others. Though it is difficult to believe Dad did not miss the money, still there was no mention of the money disappearing regularly from our family bank account. Even in confession that afternoon, he never mentioned the amount of money outgoing each month for Mom's medications. I am certain he felt guilty for allowing the entire family to suffer financially for her habit.

Three words were legal in the 1960s that helped Valium addiction explode within American suburbia. A physician could simply write "Refill as needed." A patient could then refill the Valium prescription once a month without a return to the doctor for a new script. The intent of the doctor was well-meaning. The added words helped a patient make fewer visits to the doctor, saving time and money. Furthermore, many family physicians felt inadequate to treat emotional illnesses. Since psychiatry still remained a practice in the larger cities and hospitals, many family practitioners had to serve as make-do psychiatrists out of necessity. However, many of these physicians were unaware of Valium's insidious addictive power, and that many, like my mother, learned to secure as many as six prescriptions marked "refill as needed." Therefore, Mom possessed hundreds of tablets at any given time. As her stash grew, so did her drug intake.

After Mom's death we discovered bottles of Valium, and a few narcotics stored throughout the house. As we flushed the medications away, I wondered how much money Mom spent on drugs. It was obvious from the amount of medications we discovered that Mom was headed toward death. What remained of her original personality would become lost in the false self-serving persona created by the drugs; and her body would weaken from the toxicity of the medications.

Though Mom died of a rare lung disease, her physical health diminished from years of drug use. Her body revealed Mom's weakening condition. The atrophy of her muscles left her limbs thin and frail. The skin that once covered normal muscle tone now sagged loosely from her upper arms, and it developed a slight yellowish hue. Her mouth suffered from chronic dryness and she ate glasses of crushed ice almost nonstop. Fluid retention from the intake of ice accompanied by lack of exercise affected the shape of her body. She looked "top heavy," as the fluid gathered around her stomach and her legs lost size from loss of muscle mass. In the last years we were observing the rapid deterioration of her health.

Therefore, when the illness struck, her body offered little resistance. Other individuals with the illness have lived years; yet Mom died within one month. Her will was weak, and later the autopsy revealed the damage to her organs. Mom's body and mind could not generate enough energy to fight. Drug addiction was not the stated cause of death; however, doctors admitted the years of substance abuse hastened it. I was correct that afternoon as Mom screamed at me and my teenage friend through the front door. I did eventually lose her. Our discovery of drugs throughout the house proved it inevitable.

Chapter 9

Imprisoned

"Craig, are you going to walk with me?"

"Don't worry Jenny. It will be okay."

Sadly, as soon as Dad found serenity and made peace with those he felt hurt by his actions, he passed. The visit on the porch and our blossoming friendships became cherished heirlooms for me. They are beautiful treasures that glisten in a history of tarnished opportunities. The events surrounding his death provided Dad and me with our most tender and precious moments in life, but they unhinged Jenny from life.

W.B. Yeats is among my favorite poets to read. He wrote:

Turning and turning in the widening gyre
The falcon cannot hear the falconer;
Things fall apart; the center cannot hold;
Mere anarchy is loosed upon the world.

Jenny was the falcon and Dad the falconer, and the center. After his death there was no anchor to hold Jenny from self-destruction. She was loosed upon the world, a collection of destructive memories in search of love.

In the more manic phases of Jenny's illness she spent money as though she owned a bank. In reality she owned nothing. Her coffee table was stacked with "overdrawn" warnings from the bank. She drove a used car that always appeared as though it was near its end. Jenny earned a good income through private nursing and arranging trips for older adults and church groups. We remained mystified regarding where the money went. Jenny's net worth was less than $30,000 though her income was at times almost double that amount.

When a trip she planned for an out-of-town group had to be canceled for reasons beyond Jenny's control, those who signed on wanted their refund. Jenny responded with nervous agitation. Her answers to those requesting their money became contradictory and eventually she ignored them altogether. She had good reason for her anxiety. Jenny had no money to give them. She spent it.

Though she never addressed the issue of the missing money, Penny and I deduced she loaned or gave the money to significant people in her life, especially males. A loan and gift were the same for she never received repayment. She never asked that the money be returned. We discovered Jenny loaned one male friend $4,000 with no paperwork or plan for repayment. After Jenny paid dearly for her actions, he still refused to return the money. Jenny deeply cared for him, but he could not reciprocate. She was just a friend, a good friend who would loan him money with ease. This loan was only one incident we happened to discover. Certainly there were many others. There exists no logical conclusion regarding what happened to the money. Jenny would rather face the consequences of an angry tour group than lose an individual for whom she deeply cared from her life. Jenny was still attempting to buy love.

The group came from a small town, and the leaders were embarrassed to have sent the money of dear friends to Jenny only to have the trip canceled with no refund. They hired a lawyer. Jenny eventually was arrested for fraud. In spite of almost $14,000 taken, Jenny did not even have the money to hire a lawyer and was assigned a public defender. The public defender stopped practicing law within a few weeks after Jenny's case for "personal reasons." Therefore, she had no one to see her case through the judicial system. Jenny received eight months in jail and was forced to pay full restitution. Though I was naturally biased, I felt the punishment harsh. It was Jenny's first offense and evidence was presented from psychiatrists of her bipolar illness. Since the inability to handle money is one of the symptoms of bipolar illness it is unbelievable the court did not realize a very sick woman stood before the bar. The arms of justice so broken in her childhood now grabbed her as a mentally ill adult with the full measure of its power.

Many forget that when a person is sentenced for a first crime, the judgment reaches far beyond the penalty specified by court documents. Jenny lost her nursing license, and paying the money back became an insurmountable problem. The cost of restitution within the time frame assigned placed her in a position of severe stress. If a light existed at the end of that tunnel, it was at best a speck for her.

Her response to serving time in jail was to avoid it. Jenny had suffered severe claustrophobia for years. As a nurse she refused to ride in elevators, choosing the stairs instead. Living eight months in a small jail cell was terrifying for Jenny. In response, she feigned attempting suicide. She tried losing herself in the thick woods near an interstate until hypothermia set in. The sheriff's department quickly found her after we reported her missing. They found her wild eyed, her clothes ripped and covered in mud. Red clay soiled her hands and was thick beneath her fingernails from her attempts to climb an embankment onto the interstate where she could more easily be found. She almost lost her life due to her inability to climb the bank. Thankfully the Sheriff's department looked thoroughly for her.

Jenny was trying to obtain sympathy in last ditch attempts to avoid jail. On other occasions she acted as though she were going to leap in front of a semi-truck; on two occasions she actually leaped onto the highway. The massive truck's tires squealed as the rubber burned, leaving skid marks on the road where they avoided hitting her. It was becoming less obvious that she was not seriously trying to kill herself. We had to treat every attempt as serious.

Although she initially pulled back early enough for a truck to screech to a stop, the frightened truckers were forced to report her to the authorities. On every occasion Jenny was admitted to a psychiatric unit for several days of observation, thus postponing her entering jail. Upon release she would leap again in front of a vehicle. The pattern became predictable, but always in a different location where the authorities did not know her. Therefore, she was always admitted to a different hospital.

On one occasion she employed a different method and barely escaped alive. She overdosed on a combination of prescription and over-the-counter medications and slipped into a coma. Thanks to the doctor's skill and accompanying prayers, she survived. She was taken to a drug unit, and when her insurance money ran out, she was moved to a free unit that took care of alcoholics as a ministry. Jenny was not only attempting suicides, she was drinking regularly and dangerously.

Penny and I attended the family sessions offered as part of Jenny's treatment. I couldn't help but think, "Now, after all of these years, Jenny and I are sitting together with a therapist." Jenny's choice of subject matter only inflamed my anger that no one considered our emotional health during those most painful years. Though we had now moved far down the road of life, we seemed to remain the two children in the small house wanting to scream.

Mom's hatred of Jenny was always used as the excuse. However, we knew she had to accept responsibility for stealing the money and the dangerous means she used to avoid jail. Even though Jenny used the money to buy love, still, she stole from another. Blaming Mom accomplished nothing productive or constructive for Jenny. The blame soothed her angry heart and offered a measure of solace for her conscience; but that was it.

Blame does offer benefits or we would not utilize it so frequently and determinedly. The benefits however are transient. The counselors were not buying her "poor me" story and came down hard on Jenny. Penny and I supported their attempt to awaken Jenny to the chaos she was creating not just for herself, but for others.

In those sessions I personally and adamantly reminded Jenny that she was contradicting herself. She complained that Mom unjustly hurt her, yet now she was hurting others using Mom as an excuse, which was unjust. She complained that Mom caused her suffering and it hurt, but Jenny was now causing great suffering for others without thought of the pain she was inflicting. Initially Jenny would become irate in response to my challenge, but later settled down and accepted the truth. With the help of her therapists and family, she usually left feeling better.

However, attempting to transform Jenny in the midst of severe bipolar illness exacerbated by alcoholism resulted in behavioral changes of short duration. Quickly Jenny regressed, and the old behaviors surfaced. Though we were aware that Jenny had developed a raging alcohol problem, it was far more severe than we imagined. She was drinking up to six or more beers in less than thirty minutes. Jenny wasn't drinking beer and wine, she was pouring it down her throat.

For over six months Jenny escaped serving an eight-month term in jail by moving from one psychiatric or drug addiction hospital to another. Still, the eight months in jail awaited. Penny and I tried to chase her down and force her to face the penalty. We certainly were not anxious to send our sister to jail; yet we knew the longer Jenny postponed the inevitable the more suicide attempts awaited her in the future. We were rightfully terrified that she might prove successful. Jenny's son was not initially helpful, but I understood his growing reluctance. The thought of helping send one's mother to jail would upset any child. The age of the child matters little. His mother committed the crime, but it was his "mama" he was helping to send to jail.

After her release she disappeared again. We finally located her in the panhandle of Florida. Jenny had again leaped into the path of a semi. Chris, Penny and I drove five hours to pick her up. While there she had agreed to, and underwent electroshock treatments, just as our mother had done. Upon learning of Jenny's choice to submit to the treatment, I grew deeply agitated. My irritation was exacerbated by the memory of Mom's treatment and her inability to remember my name. My mother's memory loss appeared like a terrifying ghost incarnate in Jenny. Like Mom, Jenny suffered from emotional distress, addictive disease, neglect of her child in the early years, and a stubborn refusal to change. Again, Jenny was fighting Mom by fighting against behaviors in her own life that mimicked Mom's destructive life.

The effects of Valium continued to course through the collective life of our family. Life was still chaotic; anger still brewed within each of us, though we often did not know with whom and for what specific reasons we were really angry. We were just angry at life. As Mom looked at life through a drugged, dazed reality, we were looking at life through our own hazy memories. St. Paul might say, we were a family "looking through a glass dimly."

Before leaving the Florida hospital, the psychiatrist called me aside and said, "Your sister must never marry again. As a matter of fact, she should never be with a man again. She does not know where she ends and he begins. She loses her identity in him. Her sense of self is so ill formed, the boundaries that most of us possess to define ourselves, to say 'This is me' do not exist for her. She has needed love too badly for too long."

In therapy I learned that this state is called a "symbiotic relationship." The identity of one person is so intertwined with another, or lost within the personality of a separate individual, they have no sense of their own self. In Jenny's disturbed mind there was no Jenny. The slow, steady destruction of Jenny's self-esteem eradicated the Jenny I knew in childhood and as a young adult. Although Mom was dead, Jenny was still so wrapped up in Mom's life through painful memories, she could not break free and enjoy her own life. The doctor continued his explanation to me, "Therefore, when she needs pleasure she does anything the male wants, even to the point of breaking the law." No one ever asked Jenny to break the law, of which I am aware. However, if Jenny thought more money would purchase love, she would stop at nothing. The doctor was not offering an excuse, only an explanation.

Though not a psychiatrist my Masters in Marriage and Family Therapy endowed me with the ability to understand the psychiatrist. Once we got Jenny in the car, the doors were locked down along with the windows. It was then that I informed Jenny of our destination. We spent much of the trip trying to convince her that she could survive eight months in jail. We would be with her and make sure she received care. Honestly, we were as unsure of what the future held for Jenny as Jenny.

Hours later we arrived at the jail. It had already been decided that I would walk her into the jail and stand with her as she surrendered. It was what Jenny wanted, and it was only fitting. The two of us lived imprisoned by a painful past and I needed to share her chains as we walked toward the jail. Though I found a path of sufficient light to walk through the pain of our childhood, I was still joined to Jenny in heart. Her pain was still my pain. We were inseparable siblings sharing a secretive, dark, abusive history. Only when we found a path through and out of the pain together would we know peace. I prayed Jenny would begin a new life during her time in jail. Perhaps this was the traumatic event that would transport her soul from the past into a new present and future.

I had called the sheriff ahead of time, and they were expecting us. She said tearful goodbyes to her son and Penny. I held her hand and walked through the dark night toward the single lighted window of the jail office. It was by far the most difficult walk I had ever taken. I talked every step of the way. "We are going to stand with you Jenny. I am going to see you as often as I can. You can stand these eight months and then a new life can begin." Within thirty yards I was attempting to comfort my dear sister who had suffered over thirty years of her life. What could I possibly say now?

Jenny remained calm, but I felt her squeeze my hand as we neared the door. Fortunately the deputies were kind and gentle. It was still gut-wrenching to watch them place Jenny in handcuffs. All I could see was the little girl peeping over the stove, dropping to the floor to ward off blows, and have lockets flung back at her head. I bit my lip to keep from breaking. I hugged her goodbye and promised to visit her; then, I stepped outside. I was still in sight of Penny and Chris, so I stood outside the door and fought to keep from breaking into a sob. This took several minutes. I walked on eggshells to the car, just as Jenny and I had done as children. We then drove away, leaving Jenny in a tiny cell. I glanced over my shoulder and remembered the sister waving from the window of the mental hospital.

Jenny was transferred to the jail in the county where the fraud had occurred. The family visited her as often as possible. The most memorable visit for me was at Easter. I had preached three services that morning and was exhausted. Now I sat behind a piece of plastic to talk to my sister over a phone. It was difficult to watch her approach in her jail uniform. The talk was emotional and I tried to keep her mind on the fact that only a few months remained. Yet, Jenny wanted me to know of her life in jail, not to inflict guilt, but to let those who might hate her know she was suffering. Jenny felt she needed to be punished. Her sense of shame was evident. This broke my heart, but there was little I could do for her guilt. She mentioned the jobs assigned to her. One of them was mopping the floors. Once again the memories of her cleaning the house as an eight-year old child emerged with startling clarity. It was the vision that would haunt me that entire Easter.

Easter is the celebration of resurrection. I wondered if any good could still arise from this death-like existence for Jenny. Jenny was in her own tomb. Though Jenny had broken the law and had to take responsibility, I felt deeply in my psyche that something was still very wrong with the picture. Mom's Valium addiction had served to incarcerate Jenny twice in institutions.

As we visited in the concluding months of her sentence, Jenny talked little about what occurred in jail. I think Jenny knew it upset me. Instead she spoke of the future. Many of her statements began with the words: "When I get out of here, I am going to . . ."

I believe on a deep emotional level Jenny had been using those words from her earliest years; except her heart would have worded the introduction: "When Mama loves me I am going to…"

Once again I recalled Jenny singing "Georgie Girl." She had now moved on in the song. She was looking for the "new Georgie Girl," and I prayed that she found her, and soon.

Chapter 10

Last Words

"She Always Hated Me."

"Jenny, you are right. Mom hated you and I don't know why."

We were especially proud of Jenny over the last months. Released from jail she became active in AA. She earned her six month chip for sobriety, even though the bipolar illness continued to be unmanageable. Penny, Jenny's son Chris, and our stepmother Gladys were present when Jenny proudly received the chip for six months of sobriety. I lived almost three hours away and could not attend the important event. I phoned in my congratulations; however, I would later regret not choosing to sit in the audience and give her the gift of a smile and the feel of my embrace.

As a clergyman I had learned through the years that nothing touches an individual like the presence of another; especially someone they respect and love. I never called in my prayers when a member faced serious surgery. My presence in the room, the touch of my hand upon theirs as I offered a personal prayer meant everything to the patient. In ministry we call this action "the ministry of presence." Often we need to say little, for our presence speaks volumes regarding the love and care of God expressed through the church. On this special night in Jenny's life I phoned in my love. I did the unthinkable, for I convinced myself the words spoken over the phone could convey the depth of love and care in my heart. They can't.

The night of Penny's birthday the small community in which she lived threw a night of music in her honor. Gail and I drove up along with friends. Jenny's bipolar alcoholism reared its head like a poisonous serpent and struck hard. She either smuggled alcohol into the event or found someone who acquired the alcohol for her. Regardless of how she got the alcohol, she was drunk; Jenny rarely became what I called in high school "sloppy drunk." However, she did stumble when walking and slurred her words when interacting with others. When intoxicated, Jenny always became loose tongued. Still, she could carry on a lucid, logical conversation.

Penny was angry and hurt for Jenny had taken a great night for Penny and embarrassed her. Penny deserved better. With me living so far away Penny bore much of the responsibility in caring for Jenny. "I can't deal with her! I am too angry right now!" Penny said intentionally avoiding looking at Jenny. I could not blame Penny. She had worked hard to make the evening a success, invited close friends, and instead of enjoying the music and talking with friends Penny was now hoping no one saw Jenny stumbling through the store Penny ran and the concert area outside.

I decided to intervene. Gail first noticed Jenny's slurred speech and changed mood. She warned me that Jenny could not drive; she was a danger to herself and everyone on the road. Therefore, we could not simply ask Jenny to leave. I called Jenny aside and began what would become the most important conversation we had in years; no, the most important in our life.

I had learned that when Jenny was drunk, there was a predictable process, a ritual that had to be followed if Jenny was going to listen. First, I battled her denial. Jenny always denied she was intoxicated. I listened to the customary "No I'm not! I just drank a little! I can drive home with no trouble!"

I countered with a litany of fact. "Jenny, listen! You can't speak without slurring your words. You are stumbling all over the place. We love you and cannot let you behind the wheel. It is obvious to everyone that you are drunk, Jenny!" Jenny was not listening. Like many of us, she was already planning her response instead of paying attention. Several times she tried to interrupt.

I knew allowing her to remain in denial would help her feel better about herself. If anyone needed a good shot of self-esteem it was Jenny. Yet, I also knew if I surrendered to her denial I was telling Jenny she wasn't worth the argument. Once sober again, she would know exactly what my unwillingness to fight meant. It is a tedious and wearisome task to argue with a drunk. One must be prepared to go the distance, to repeat the same truths over and again, and to be so determined to win, that your opponent becomes the first to grow weary. I knew Jenny's thought processes well. If I stayed the course Jenny would know I loved her. I could not allow the repetitive denials to frustrate me.

I continued to counter her illogical denials by pointing out the obvious symptoms of her intoxication. "You smell like a distillery. You have miscounted the money. You have almost fallen three times." I continued this assault on her denial and eventually won. Sadly, I did not realize that I was raising my voice to counter Jenny's arguing, and it was upsetting Penny. So I took the argument outside the store.

Why was I raising my voice? I was not aware of the increase in volume. I spoke not only loudly, but irately. My words were soused with anger. Jenny stiffened and stumbled back, attempting to distance herself from me. It was then that I realized my attempt to help Jenny was in fact frightening her. Obviously, my anxiety level soared; but that was understandable. No one enjoys confronting an intoxicated sister. Still, I sensed the stress was rising from that deep place in the soul where our darkest emotions are assigned.

The rage stored so deeply in my soul, the rage I considered dead and buried was then flashing in my eyes and spewing from my mouth. I wasn't angry at Jenny for being drunk; I was irate at having to talk with Jenny on such a vulnerable level. Jenny was the one person in my life that made me most susceptible to emotional pain. Forced to look her in the eye and confront her drinking meant skirting around the painful past we shared. I was well acquainted with the journey that brought us to that moment outside the store. Thank God Jenny stopped her denials. My anger, I am convinced, frightened her into silence. Regaining my composure I suppressed all thoughts related to our past and concentrated again on taking care of Jenny.

She at last admitted drinking to the point of "being high." Jenny refused to use the word drunk. Still, her admission to being disoriented and unable to drive was important. Now Jenny entered the second phase of the ritual: shame, a difficult stage to confront. Jenny was quite pitiful when feeling ashamed. I needed to say little. Over the years Jenny had sadly learned to inflict herself with plenty of shame. As a matter of fact, she was far too tough on herself when she failed. What little self-worth remained in her life was in shreds. I knew walking softly through her shame was vital for her wellbeing. My role had to become that of the comforting brother. "Listen Jenny, you just fell tonight. They told you in AA that these moments would be possible, if not probable. We love you, and we will help you begin again. This night must be forgotten. Let us get you into bed, go to sleep, and tomorrow you will feel better. I promise things will look better tomorrow than they do now. You can attend an AA meeting. Everyone can start over Jenny." As a minister, and from my experiences in life, I believed in that truth. The most basic and powerful truth of Christianity is that resurrection can follow the darkest pain. I knew Jenny believed this truth as well; however, she struggled to embrace it for herself. I had to almost convince Jenny she was worth a second chance. Again, I knew why she struggled to believe a second chance was in her future. I wanted to move on, and quickly; for I felt old memories stirring.

Jenny did not answer, or speak at all. She simply cried. I wasn't sure she heard all I said, but she heard enough. Jenny felt shame deeply, but she also had learned to fight when too much shame was heaped upon her by someone else. Suddenly the eyes that cried sparked with fire. She was moving into the next stage that I hated. I had talked Jenny through this next stage so often I was afraid my words would be ineffective.

Jenny raised herself from shame to deep anger, for now she engaged in blame and the momentary strength it provided. "You know Mama loved you more than me! She hated me!" Jenny launched into a tirade against the same person she always blamed, our mother. One of the reasons I hated this stage so deeply was that it was filled with a great deal of truth. So much of what Jenny said was true, and I, more than anyone, knew it.

Still, I knew blame did nothing for Jenny; it only reinforced the psychological damage and pain Jenny knew too well. "Jenny, no one made you drink tonight. It was your choice. Come on Jenny, who held you down and poured it into your mouth?" Jenny attempted to interrupt with another vicious attack on Mom. I was speaking hard and fast. I learned this line of questioning during my clinical training in an alcohol treatment facility.

Though my words were predictable, they proved successful. Jenny always surrendered during this phase; not because she believed Mom was innocent, but because Jenny was smart enough to know that blame was useless in making her feel better. I helped her realize she was still allowing Mom to make her miserable if she drank. In the short term the blame offered Jenny catharsis; in the long term it offered nothing but painful memories. I did not know just how alone Jenny felt in those memories. I was too concerned, far too concerned with protecting my own heart.

Having reached the conclusion that blame was not helpful, Jenny digressed into shame again. However, she did not revisit this state for a lengthy period of time. By this time she was tired and weary of the debate. She accepted the fact that she was intoxicated, could not drive, and needed sleep. Penny found Jenny a bed for the night. I drove her there and helped her settle in.

The conversation that was needed for years now started in earnest. I always told Jenny I loved her. We never left one another without saying those words. However, this night was different. The words were the same, but they too were arising from that place in the soul where both of us ached. "Jenny, you know if I didn't love you, I wouldn't say the things I do. I just wouldn't care."

"I know," she spoke softly.

"Jenny, you are right. Mom hated you, and I don't know why." It was the first time I had spoken this truth out loud to Jenny. Previously I had always assumed it would not help her. Now I realized that perhaps she needed to hear someone agree with her, someone who had been there, witnessed it, and most importantly believed it happened. I was that person. Immediately I grew teary. I was surprised at how quickly my emotions were stirred when I admitted that truth to Jenny. The dam was beginning to break.

When I acknowledged that Mom hated her, and there was no other word to use and no means of softening that painful reality, something in me recognized that Jenny had suffered more deeply than I wanted to believe. I did more than validate Jenny's suffering, I validated the painful fact that I had lived it with her. I entered into my own sense of guilt and shame, for it was now painfully obvious that for over forty plus years I had said nothing. Our psyches were screaming, and I said nothing. Jenny had tried to engage me in a dialogue about the past. I dismissed her attempts as unhelpful, as adding pain upon pain. The greater pain lived in my silence, and the absence of a conversation about a shared past that damaged both of us. The New Testament book of James encourages us to confess our sins to one another that we might "be healed." However, honestly confessing truth in any fashion is healing. Jenny wanted to do just that; I did not.

I continued to speak emotionally and fluidly to Jenny as the questions raced through my mind, "I don't know why she loved me and abused you; and that's what it was Jenny, abuse." The words "hate" and "abuse" I had never spoken in relation to our childhood and our mother. "I did care Jenny, I really did." I was now teary. For the first time ever, I was unlocking the door, the door that opened into the dark memories that terrified me. Behind that door lived a myriad of painful events, numerous questions, and more answers to those questions than I wanted to acknowledge. I realized Jenny and I were walking toward that dark abyss of our shared past as we talked. I admit, initially I wanted to turn and run, run with every ounce of energy I possessed. However, deep within myself I was strangely drawn toward the darkness. Perhaps this was the beginning. Yes, now Jenny and I would at last talk. Love could fully spring to life and we could at last enjoy the beauty of just being together!

Jenny also felt the emotional connection we had shared since childhood. "I know it wasn't easy for you either," she said, almost as if she needed to say one more thing before retiring. I looked at her in shock. These were words she had never said. "I will never forget that Christmas when Daddy beat you so badly." As soon as she said it the memory rushed to life. It was a memory I had long ago buried. I had to, for emotional self-preservation. The scene played in my mind with startling clarity as she spoke.

Jenny was crying after reminding me of that painful event. She knew how badly it hurt me, and knew that I understood the abuse she endured all her life. I had experienced moments of painful behavior; Jenny had experienced a lifetime. That night we both acknowledged the very truth I spent my entire adulthood struggling to avoid, the truth that Jenny struggled to overcome. The childhood we shared, that made us too uncomfortable to sit in the same room more than an hour, had been admitted, confessed. It was real, destructive and shared. Now healing could begin.

Before leaving Jenny we hugged and shared words of love. We did not want to visit our childhood further that night. It was too tiring and painful. Yet, we had taken a giant leap forward in restoring our life as siblings. I looked in my rear view mirror as I left to make sure Jenny did not leave the room. I wanted her to sleep. I had never been more hopeful about the two of us than that evening. For the first time we could help each other find healing; and that journey would bind us together with renewed strength. I looked over my shoulder, and for the first time looked forward to seeing her again, and soon.

As stated, we were a family that loved popular music. Our conversation filled me with hope, the hope that we could break free from the past and fully become the people God intended. I listened for Jenny's childish voice singing the lyrics of her favorite song.

Initially I wanted to cry, "Yes! I want the world to see a new Jenny!" Then I realized I really wanted the world to see the old Jenny, the beautiful, loving child that lived and entertained me before abuse created so much pain that Jenny stopped living and starting surviving. The time for hiding was over. "Yes Jenny! Let's bring out all the love we hide and 'O what a change there will be!'"

Chapter 11

Unfinished Business

"No, not Jenny!"

The phone rang. I walked into the room with Gail after she answered. It was my last walk of strength for months.

The latter part of May our telephone rang at home. We lived three hours south of Juliette. Juliette is a charming little town, famed for having most of the movie *Fried Green Tomatoes* filmed there. Penny and her friend Robin lived and worked there in a little shop we owned together. Behind the shop was the site of the concert for Penny's birthday. The phone call was from Juliette.

My wife Gail answered the call. Gail possesses one of the most authentic southern voices I've heard in life. As an authentic son of the Deep South that is a grandiose claim. Nevertheless, I believe I speak truthfully. Gail's words roll off her tongue like thick sweet honey. The tone and choice of her words express charm and sincere interest in the life of the one with whom she converses. However, within seconds I intuitively sensed the telephone call heralded some dark, foreboding news. The honey-like drawl was present, but her tone was far too flat, actually it was sad. Penny had called. She and Gail usually engaged in upbeat chatty conversation. This May evening Gail spoke few words and was far too quiet. Then, I heard those expressions that serve as the prelude to tragic news. "O no! When? How did it happen?"

Instinctively I rose from the recliner and walked into the bedroom. My mother died at age 46, and I had recently lost my father. I was not prepared for another loss; but who is? When Gail laid the phone on her shoulder and faced me, her face appeared ashen. "Craig, Jenny killed herself this afternoon." There was no way to convey that news other than speaking the blunt facts. How does one decorate or embellish such news? For the first time in life I literally had to steady myself. As a clergyman for thirty years I comforted many who became unsteady when losing a loved one. Now the room spun and my legs felt rubbery. I was not a clergyman; I was a brother with the emotional and spiritual wind knocked from him. I grabbed the dresser and braced for her to finish delivering the news. My mind was so consumed by a single thought I became lost in it. I was lost in grief, lost in pictures of Jenny taking her life racing through my head. The natural laws that governed all things seemed suspended.

Jenny locked the store, walked one mile down the railroad track of Juliette, and threw herself into the path of a speeding train. Had destructive fate said, "Hey, you again?" Or, was God powerless to stop my sick sister from such an horrendous act of violence against herself? Too many questions screamed in my emotional ears. The destructive, personal universe Jenny and I shared as children had at last collapsed upon itself. The one clear truth ringing in my ears over the next few days was that our childhood had never reached its end. Jenny lived it all the way to the railroad tracks.

I belong to a group of clergy named "The Order." We are deeply committed and accountable to one another. Without hesitation they offered a memorial service for Jenny. The Methodist Home for Children and Youth provided their chapel for the service. The Home had embraced Jenny for the last years, and Jenny had a great appreciation for their ministries to children. The day of the memorial I realized why Jenny loved the Home. I believe Jenny wished such a place existed when she was a child.

We were more grateful than we could possibly express, for we could not think clearly. Having someone take the lead, who is capable and caring, was an answer to prayer. I have seven fellow ministers who are brothers to me. We love and care deeply for one another. They immediately opened their hearts and arms and acted. We were still dealing with the news trickling out into the community. Initially we were hurt by a newspaper that really attempted to help us. The paper did not print the horrible story of Jenny's suicide. Instead they only printed that she was walking along the track and was struck by a train. Really, they could print little else for the autopsy had yet to be done, and the findings of Law Enforcement were not yet revealed. In a section of the paper entitled "Rant and Rave" individuals can write anything without signing their name. Some wrote horrible criticisms of Jenny without knowing the full story. Jenny was ripped in the paper by a small few for being "stupid." She was being chastised in death for not having better sense than to walk along a railroad track in the early evening. Though they were few, it still hurt us. I had to "forgive them, for they did not know what they were doing."

When Jenny's remains were released, we met with the funeral home in Forsyth, Georgia; they were more than compassionate. Immediately they pleaded with us not to ask questions about the body. In other words, the body was so destroyed not even the funeral home wanted to explain the condition of the body. We agreed together the only thing to do was to cremate the remains. One of the directors of the funeral home told us that a ring was on Jenny's finger, but there was no way to get it off. It would have to be cremated as well. One of the family arrived late at the funeral home and heard only that bit of explanation. She asked, "Why can't we get the ring off?" The face of the director said everything. We never asked about the body again.

After the autopsy, we planned a private, family gathering to spread Jenny's ashes where we assumed she would prefer. As I watched the ashes blow in the wind the enormity of what had

happened throughout Jenny's life hit me. It took all the emotional
strength I had to remain strong, especially for Chris, Jenny's son.
He helped spread the ashes with little emotion. I knew a ticking
bomb was going to blow in his psyche. Losing his mom to suicide
hurt him, I knew it. Chris is a sweet, sensitive young man. Two
weeks later he ran into his back yard and emotionally broke. He
then began the process of healing.

Initially it was believed that Jenny left us without a suicide
note. Yet, the more I mourned her death, and her choice in dying,
the greater grew my awareness of her "implied note." Jenny's note
was in her method. When Jenny died, she felt as though she faced
a trainload of demands and requirements that had become
impossible to handle. Her life was running over her, and she said
exactly that on those railroad tracks.

Secondly, Jenny owned little or no sense of identity. Jenny
felt like dirt her entire life, and said so. Her self worth was ripped
to shreds from childhood until death. When Jenny threw herself in
the path of the train, there was no body for us to bury. There was
no "identifiable Jenny." We released her ashes to the wind. I
watched tearfully as they blew freely away. The family would now
begin to emotionally let go of the pain related to Jenny's death.
However, Jenny's memory and means of death were not letting go
of me. Not then, not now, not ever. I alone knew why she walked
to those tracks.

PART III

THE FINISH
OR
THE START?

Chapter 12

Regret

The suicide was the end of Jenny and me, other than the afterlife. Our story was over. There was no comma marking the next step for us out of the destructive flow of history, only a heart-wrenching period. There was no place to go with this journey, other than to walk in depressive regret. For weeks after Jenny's suicide I lived imprisoned by the worst form of sorrow. Regret slammed the door of opportunity on us. When I drove away from Jenny hoping we could begin a walk toward healing, I assumed many opportunities awaited us. I didn't realize tomorrow wasn't coming.

Jenny was dead. I would never see her again in this life; our relationship had no nice, tidy ending. Our history ended with unfinished business. So much that needed to be said and done would never transpire. When imprisoned by regret, we become immersed in a *hypothetical world*. We are haunted by the unanswerable question, "What if?" Though I knew my answers were nothing but conjecture, I could not stop interrogating myself. A mind captivated by the hypothetical is a mind wasted. We are failing to deal with the issues at hand because we cannot deal with the issues of the past, especially when they are incomplete.

I believe many children from homes where substance abuse creates loss tend to blame themselves. As I continued to struggle with the hypothetical questions, they became very personal. I was now asking, "Why didn't I do something?" "Why didn't I talk when I had the opportunity?" The most painful question that emerged in the interrogation was, "Could I have saved Jenny's life?" Blame and guilt had become my constant companions.

Why shouldn't I feel guilty? I had countless opportunities to talk with Jenny, and I didn't. There were moments when her body language and even her words were pleading for me to talk with her. I didn't. Therefore, when she took her life, I began to assume responsibility. With each passing day I disliked myself even more. At this point I was beginning to believe there was no answer to the regret I felt.

I sought my friend and mentor Dr. Edwin Chase, a family therapist with The Methodist Home for Children and Youth, and articulated my feelings. In his usual calm, caring manner he allowed me to finish expressing the guilt and shame that was plunging me ever deeper into depression. Then he asked me a pointed, powerful question, "Craig, don't you think if you could have saved Jenny, you would?" His questions and comments that afternoon allowed me to own a true sense of arrogance. It is rare that realizing you are arrogant helps you feel better, but it did.

I was choosing to believe that I was well, strong and complete. When I thought of the past, it was always with Jenny as the one needing help and me being the only one that could save her. Dr. Chase helped me realize that I wasn't as strong as I liked to think. I didn't talk with Jenny because it just hurt too badly. My strength was more imaginary than real. I had not dealt with the past any more than Jenny. It is for this reason that I avoided her. I could not stand to even think about yesterday. In retrospect I can see my own brokenness. The strength to deal with the past just wasn't there. I couldn't rescue Jenny because I needed help myself. I recalled a statement I made in our story. "Jenny and I left childhood as damaged goods." Both of us moved into adolescence broken and hurting.

I then had to confront the question, "Am I just trying to absolve myself of responsibility, or am I really that broken?" It was a legitimate question. This question was not answered overnight. Over the next months I wrestled with this question with fervor. If ever I needed a question answered, it was this one. The answer to the question was going to be painful. If I was healthy and had moved on with my life, then I was responsible. If I was broken and filled with loss, I needed help. For a minister and counselor for over thirty years, neither answer was beneficial for my ego strength. I am convinced that many from homes of substance abuse blame themselves for the brokenness and loss that continued throughout life. Trying to help them realize that they did not have the power they assumed and were as needy as anyone is not an easy sell.

Substance abuse that leads to various forms of loss and death tend to leave the children from that home in such quandaries. How can we move on in life if we do not believe in our own inner strength? If that emotional and spiritual power we count on daily lacks substance and is weak, we are left with inadequacy. We must then admit that we are still victims of the past. God, no wonder there is so much pain and dysfunction in later life! I did not realize at the time that only through admitting my own pain and need could I really move forward in my life.

During this time of soul searching, I was comforted by my belief in the afterlife. God promised to "wipe away all tears." I was certain that in eternity Jenny and I would know the beauty of reconciliation. Though I found comfort in my faith, it still did not eradicate my painful sorrow. The promise of hope in eternity was not enough to remove the sting of regret in the here and now. Since eternity was about the future, what was I to do in the here and now? Where was I to go with my pain and restlessness? How do you move onward toward any destination when life sticks a period in your story when you expect a comma? Initially I could not answer these questions. Still, I knew that I had to find an escape from the regret. I was emotionally wasting away in that dark cell.

I prayed for light to burst into my prison and offer hope. The hope that the story could continue in spite of Jenny's death was the key I needed to unlock the door. If our childhood could serve as light for others from homes of addiction, if it could offer a message of hope for the addict and her children, then the period would be removed. New chapters could be written and move our story toward a sense of purpose. This was the direction my life needed to take. The path toward healing for me was not "the road less traveled," but rather the "road already traveled."

Did light exist in our painful story? Naturally, light was present in those flashes of normality and in the moments of laughter and joy. But, was there light in the pain? Our life together teemed with far too much pain, and I could never move onward in life unless the pain itself could offer hope. The sorrow itself needed to speak, and its message had to be one of light.

If I was going to connect with that light, it would be in our "story." Karen Armstrong, in the Sept. 12–13, 2009 edition of the *Wall Street Journal*, noted that stories are an important way we emotionally connect with truth, which is why the sacred texts of many faiths contain so many narratives. Stories appeal to more than reason; they appeal to the heart. Sometimes it is less important to argue whether or not a story is true, but whether there is truth in the story. I would need to revisit the honest events of our life and seek the truth *within them.*

Thankfully, as a person of faith I believed light was omnipresent. In human experience we possess no reality called "utter darkness." For true darkness to exist, a vacuum would have to be created that removed every light particle from within and kept every particle out. Creating darkness is impossible. Therefore, light exists at all times, in all places and in all circumstances. Darkness has nothing to do with the absence of light, but instead with whether or not there are enough particles for the eye to see.

If we enter the darkest room imaginable, we will immediately suffer a form of temporary blindness. However, if we remain still and patiently wait, eventually our pupils will enlarge. Over the next few minutes they will enlarge enough to receive the light particles present in the room. It is then that the forms and shapes of objects begin to appear. Soon we can find our way to the door and escape. Yes, light existed in our pain. I needed to walk into the darkness, withstand the momentary fear that comes from the inability to see, and patiently wait. Eventually my spiritual eyes would receive the light. That light could appear in the form of a lesson learned or a message to be shared.

And the light would have to be experienced within the darkness. I realized that I would never discover the hope and truth in our story unless I emotionally engaged that story. I could not encounter the truth by remaining emotionally detached. I would need to *feel* the emotional power of the event, let it draw me in. When we stand as closely as possible to our painful memories, it is then that we can see the light and truth that dwells there. Authorities on grief, Elizabeth Kubler-Ross and David Kessler agree that the person without closure, caught in the arms of regret, needs to emotionally revisit his story. Only then can that person gain a new perspective and greater understanding.

Granted, some events in the past are shrouded in such dense pain the light particles they hold are very few and scattered. Seeing light in these moments requires a tremendous amount of time and energy. There are some experiences so immersed in pain we may be unable to see their light in this lifetime. Still, the fact that light exists in all pain demands that we search. Again, the only alternative is to remain in painful, depressive regret. A visit to the past just might offer the message of hope and purpose we need to move into life; then we have something to say, something worth doing.

After writing the story shared in this book, I revisited it over and again. I prayerfully remained with some of my most painful recollections. In the end, I realized the light and message of our story yielded its greatest light and truth when I stepped back and considered the whole. Yes, there were truths in specific events. However, collectively our story offered its most powerful message of hope.

Chapter 13

Encountering the Light

As a child from a home of addiction and abuse, I shared our story from the perspective of *what I lost.* I looked at my mother from this perception of loss. We did lose her personality over the years and I grieve losing the mother of my childhood. The emotional distance I felt between me and my father represented the loss of quality years together. I remain sad that so much of his time and energy were invested in caring for my mother. It may have helped her, but to me it was time lost. This litany of losses runs like a scarlet cord throughout my history. There is the loss of friends, self-worth, time, health and even life.

As I recalled these painful events, I tried to examine them from every perspective possible. I asked, "What was Mom possibly feeling?" "I wonder how Dad felt." "How do I remember Jenny in that moment?" "How would outsiders have interpreted it?"

From this string of losses a precious particle of light appeared and touched me deeply. In spite of all the pain inflicted and the losses experienced, *love was present.* I knew my father loved our family. From sacrificing his career in baseball to his tearful confession on the back porch, our history revealed a caring man caught in a difficult, confusing and terrifying environment. Though praise was difficult for him to express, it did not mean it was not felt. The past taught me that not every emotion is expressed in words. Yes, he was the father standing along the fence. But, there were other places he could have been. For that matter, I realized he was always around.

One of the most liberating truths was the fact that I loved Jenny. I always had. It was love that made me turn ill when I witnessed her being abused. Love led me to pray she could find a new life outside of home. In love I chased her from one hospital to the next, sat with her in family therapy from one alcoholic treatment center to the next, walked with her into jail and hugged her in genuine hope after sharing our last words. Just as importantly, I remembered that Jenny loved me. She respected me and looked up to me her entire life. I needed to see this light of love. No, it did not eradicate all of the regret I felt, but it did begin to loosen its grip upon my life.

I did remember Mom's love for me. Mom loved me beyond measure. This was a truth I always knew. However, it did not yet appear to me as light. Her abuse of Jenny would not allow me to fully embrace her love for me. Justified or not, I still feel a large measure of guilt when I think of Mom's preferential love toward me. I pray one day I will be able to appreciate this affection.

Certainly a scarlet cord of pain winds its way in and through my life. However, there is this beautiful thread of love. Though it does not remove the pain, it makes it more bearable, on occasion more understandable. I made the statement that there was not one day in my relationship with my mother without the influence of drugs. Now I can also say that love was also present, in some way or form, to some degree, every day of my life. Yes, my life is filled with losses, but also with love.

I also considered the many friends lost through the years. For a period in the middle years of my childhood faces seemed to move in and out regularly. By the time we entered adolescence, very few friends were even made. Many of these I grieve, and I know Jenny felt the loss as well. These were people we visited. We got out of our house through visits and played. As these friends disappeared, we became isolated in our own house.

As I revisited the past, I began to recall those friendships that never left. They were few, but they were strong. Though I have no recollection of intervention by them, it doesn't mean they did not try. I cannot say with absolute certainty that a word was not spoken here and there. I do know the response it would have invoked. Mom was never receptive to outside intervention and resented efforts to help Jenny. Dad was in turn hesitant to confront Mom. Still, these friends were always present and remained in touch. For them I am deeply grateful. In light of the many who left, the few become very precious.

I remain certain that many other gifts live in my past. From my Aunt Joyce's house, where I learned that a family could live happily, without everyday tension, to the more "regular days" of our childhood, I was learning to cast my eyes toward these expressions of hope and not just upon the pain. Like treasures hidden just beneath the surface, the other gifts and loving expressions of life awaited my discovery. Again, they do not erase the many losses and the pain suffered. Still, the awareness of each gift lessens the sting of loss. Certainly Jenny's suicide will continue to break my heart. I doubt the grief from her death will ever disappear. Therefore, knowing friends and love were present in Jenny's life removes some of the sting. The memories I have of Jenny laughing and smiling help me to remember that there were moments and people she greatly enjoyed.

Children from homes of addiction always face loss. As a matter of fact, loss is a certainty. If intervention does not occur, along with the addict's embracing sobriety, death is certain. Drugs are just too toxic, especially when taken at such dosages. Our story encourages these children to look for the gifts in the darkness. They are there. It is far better to find gifts of love and support in the presence of life than in the darkness of death.

Not only did I think of my past in terms of loss, I also believed our past had nothing to say. It was a history to be mourned, not to be shared. Therefore, the fact that it is recorded here means that I discovered a message in our story. A past that warns can be an instrument of light and hope as much as the nicest family history. The story of our family is a helpful siren of warning. Believe me, we need to hear the warnings in life, as a gift.

The first warning I heard stung. As I stated, I had been asking myself "Could I have helped Jenny?" or "Was I too broken to help her?" Our story hit me over and again like a boxer's body shots. It was knocking the emotional and spiritual wind out of me. At times recalling an event was so upsetting I had to stop and leave the past alone for days at a time. Without doubt, I was bleeding. I had never stopped. The wounds still ran deep, and they were vicious. I would say to anyone in my position, "If you can't *honestly* revisit the past with a measure of comfort and strength, you are still in pain." The warning I heard was to stop believing I had mastered the past. Every moment of upset, each time I intentionally left my memories because they were too painful and every tear that welled in my eyes blared in my ears, "You are not yet whole." I believe in some way I always knew this to be true. Accepting it was another matter. Now, I would have to admit and embrace the truth. No, I couldn't help Jenny. I couldn't even help myself. The only thing I was skilled at doing was "not thinking about the past." Staying busy, being on the run and, most importantly, serving as a clergyman caring for others helped me do just that. However, chronic pain, finally won and I could no longer run from my memories, especially from Jenny's death.

Now when I walked into the past there was no diversion, no interference. The past could at long last speak, and speak clearly and truthfully. It warned me to stop running and accept the man that I am. If he's broken, he's broken. Only as I embraced him could he walk toward healing. Jenny and I both needed healing, but we could not heal each other. There was the painful fallacy that was ripping my heart apart with grief and blame. The blame slowly dissipated as I began to admit my own insufficiency. Have I found wholeness through visiting the past? No, not yet. But for the first time, I know the necessary destination; I know the man who needs to take that journey. That man is the little boy listening to Beatles records to drown the pain. He is the boy idolizing his father and missing him. He is the boy that deeply loved his mother, yet despised her. He is the boy that, along with Jenny, was just surviving the best he could.

I am thankful our story yielded this warning. If it remained unheard, I would still go through life blaming myself for Jenny's death while choosing to believe my shoulders are big enough to carry the weight of the world. My shoulders are narrow, very narrow. I can only carry my own brokenness right now. But, that's okay. That is the first step of my journey toward genuine wholeness.

I encourage any adult that left a painful past behind to hear the siren. Perhaps you have moved onward in strength. I am truly thankful. But every child from such a home must ask himself if he is running from his memories. Again, if an honest visit to the past is frightening or the last thing you want to do, it is possible that you, like me, still walk through life with enormous pain stuffed into the psyche. It is baggage that one day will become too heavy to carry through life. I have started unpacking mine, looking at the pieces and finally storing them in a healthy place, a place other than my own heart.

Our childhood story also warns loudly and clearly those parents using or abusing drugs who have children. If you believe your child is unaware of your use, or is too young to be affected, you are wrong, dead wrong. When we use and abuse drugs for non-medical reasons, we place our children upon altars of sacrifice. We may be unaware that we are sacrificing their childhood. We are destroying their joy for life, filling them instead with caution and fear. The fear and paranoia Jenny and I experienced are possible for all children in such homes. Why would anyone risk the emotional and perhaps even physical welfare of their children for an artificial experience of euphoria?

What can we do for our children when there is parental drug use in their home? Stop. That's it. Attempts to protect or shield them from substance abuse will not work. Children are not only very inquisitive, they are strongly intuitive. What they cannot say or describe, they still feel. Again, drug abuse walks in only one direction: toward death. It naturally follows that any path to death is filled with other losses. A family cannot experience these losses without their children being damaged. The children are going to be hurt, and hurt for life. That, I promise.

When the parents refuse to act on behalf of the children, I pray friends of that family will intervene. Yes, you may lose your friends, but you will save the children. I try to avoid hypothetical questions about our past. Still, I can't help but ask if Jenny might have been saved early in life through family therapy. Remember, we saw no therapist until Jenny was taken to a mental institution. The next time we sat together in family therapy came almost 40 years later, after my sister tried to take her life. The years lived without therapy allowed us to continue living adrift, trying to survive. However, in the end Jenny didn't.

Today states have a Department of Family and Children Services, or an organization that serves the same purpose. Children exposed to drug abuse by their parent can be reported anonymously to these organizations. They, in turn, are in touch with reputable counselors and institutions that can help the child.

Many members of the clergy are aware of church-related institutions of help. The clergy are required to keep this information confidential. Therefore, the reader should be able to talk with his minister without fear of being exposed for reporting. For example, in our area of Georgia, the United Methodist Church supports one of the most effective and caring institutions for abused children in the nation. The Methodist Home for Children and Youth has professionally trained counselors and social workers. Ninety percent of the children for whom they care have been exposed to drug use by their parent or parents. The Methodist Home works on saving the entire family from the effects of substance abuse. They have received national awards and recognition as one the most well-equipped, purpose-driven institutions for children. Furthermore, they treat children who are non-Methodist. We need intervention, and we need these agencies and institutions. Many other church-related centers exist for children. If we care about the children in such a home, we are without excuse for seeing that the child receives help and treatment.

If this help is withheld, reread the journey Jenny and I made through life. Even prior to our birth, the opportunity to live a full life was slipping away. We can only guess what might have happened if agencies such as the Department of Family and Children's Services and The Methodist Home for Children and Youth existed for Jenny and me. As stated earlier, I truly believe this is why Jenny felt such a connection with The Methodist Home as an adult. The fact that she was eulogized in their chapel was not lost on me. In a nationally recognized institution for helping children, my sister was remembered after living and dying without help.

Our story is again a siren of warning. It offers a painful picture of where drug abuse takes a family, and it issues a challenge for those within reach of the family. Help can be received, and lives saved. There is light in the story, and light from the story. Like a searchlight on a dark evening, our losses and pain ask for your eye, your attention and, most importantly, your response.

This effort has become the driving purpose that emerged from our childhood history. Our story is here to educate families and communities about the hidden epidemic of children suffering in homes of substance abuse. And it is an epidemic. Statistics reveal that one out of four children lives in homes of substance abuse by their parents; eight million are under age eleven. Seventy nine percent of child welfare workers claim that substance abuse is the major cause of abuse for children.

Though Valium has proved to be highly addictive with severe withdrawal symptoms making detoxification difficult, and a half-life longer than most drugs, it is still the most prescribed drug in America. News Anchor Jim Jensen shared after kicking his cocaine addiction that he was unable to overcome his addiction to Valium. It is most often prescribed for non-medical, social reasons. In other words, it is the number-one medication prescribed for stress and anxiety. One in ten adults in America takes Valium according to the U.S. Library of Medicine.

Since a large population of Americans takes Valium, it has made it unofficially an *acceptable drug*. For those who choose to

believe Valium is fine to take regularly, read our story again!
Deaths from the adverse effects of all medications are as high as
automobile accidents in America.   Therefore, on the basis of
statistical inference Valium is dangerous when used without proper
oversight and restrictions.   Herein lies the danger.   Those
susceptible to Valium addiction do not want oversight and learn
how to circumvent restrictions.

With slightly over 25% of American children living in
homes with at least one parent abusing drugs, there is a high
probability the reader directly or indirectly knows one of these
children.   These are the children of whom we are aware.
Remember, children from homes of addiction are often forced to
live in secrecy.   Therefore, that number is really higher.   If a
disease struck 25% of our children, the Center for Disease Control
would announce an epidemic. When Americans learned that those
suffering in the epidemic are children, a public outrage would
follow.   Therefore, this is a "silent epidemic."   Most of us are
unaware that a quarter of our children are watching a parent use
drugs or suffering from a parent's erratic behavior. The income of
that family will suffer, as well as the quality time that those parents
spend with their children, and over time the self-worth of those
children is ripped to shreds.   They become isolated and alone,
afraid to bring friends home. Their real fear is what their friends
might see, as well as the consequences for the child should the
friends see.

Since so many of us are unaware of this epidemic, we have
not educated our communities about children caught in their
parent's addiction. The "Just Say No" campaign made a dramatic
difference in both America's drug use and our perception of the
problem. We realized we had a drug abuse epidemic. Yet, we
never asked the question, "What is happening to the children of the
addicts?" The emphasis of "Just Say No" was focused upon the
addict and user. The family was addressed, but secondarily. We
heard, and therefore learned, very little about the children living in
these homes.

This book is written to cry, "What about us?!"   The
organization Alcoholics Victorious list on their web page many

specific ways children from homes of substance abuse suffer. The National Organization of Substance Abuse and Mental Health Services names the same consequences. This list was compiled from the organization's experience and study. Since Jenny and I experienced all of them, it is accurate to state that this is the way eighty million children are suffering. I pray after reading our story, you would never wish this upon your children or the children down the street.

If you are part of a treatment center for teen and adult addiction, please do not forget the small children in the home. When you know, or even guess, there are children living in homes where substance abuse is occurring, report it. Never take chances with the lives of children. Finally, I pray as a nation we will educate our communities that we have a national epidemic. At present it remains hidden. As long as communities give little thought to children suffering in this epidemic, kids will continue to exit childhood carrying unimaginable loss and a wealth of painful memories in their hearts.

Afterword

Regaining the Music

At Jenny's death the music stopped. The off-key voice singing "Georgie Girl" was silenced. I didn't think I'd ever hear Jenny's voice again. After finding light, hope and purpose in our story, the music returned. While driving to speak at a church, I heard new pop sensation Susan Boyle sing the song "Proud." Gail looked over at me and noticed tears trickling down my cheeks. "You're thinking about Jenny aren't you?" I was. One line in particular broke my heart for I heard Jenny cry in it.

Boyle sang, "Say I'm someone in your eyes, it's all I wanted to be." Somewhere there is a child who sings with a broken heart. There are others forbidden to sing because it gets on someone's nerves. I pray that you remember and pray for every child in homes of addiction. Help them find their song of serenity.

PART IV

ADDITIONS

Resources and Suggested Reading

There are several resources below of particular interest. Fine's *No Time to Say Goodbye: Surviving the Suicide of a Loved One* was a book I found particularly helpful with the issues of regret and closure as they relate to suicide. Strong's *An Empowering Collection by and for Teens and Adults with Bipolar Disorder, Depression and Other Neurological Brain Disorders: or 'Hidden Disabilities'* is one of the better helps for understanding loved ones with bipolar disease because many with the disease contributed to the contents. Kubler-Ross and Kessler's *On Grief and Grieving* is very helpful in dealing with the issues of regret and closure, especially when the loved one dies unexpectedly and the time for making amends seems gone. In Moe's *Understanding Addiction and Recovery Through a Child's Eyes -- Hope, Help, and Healing for Families* the reader will find assistance in seeing addiction from a child's point of view. Most books look at addiction from a "professional perspective," and it is always helpful to attempt to adopt a child's point of view. "Parental

Substance Abuse A Major Factor in Child Abuse and Neglect" is an outstanding article for recognizing the stunning number of children destructively affected by parental drug abuse. The article connects substance abuse and child abuse and does not treat them as two separate problems. The web site "Samsha" is the best clearinghouse for researching every avenue related to drug abuse. It has a valuable number of informative links that run the gamut from offering information about the effects of addiction to treatment centers. It is a "one stop" site for examining all the issues related to addiction.

Books and Articles

Allen, Jill. "Helping Children with Addicted Parents." *Metro Family Magazine*, 2010. www.metrofamilymagazine.com

Anglada, Tracy. *Intense Minds: Through the Eyes of Young People with Bipolar Disorder*. Trafford Publishing: 2006.

Black, Claudia, Ph.D. *My Dad Loves Me: My Dad Has a Disease, A Child's View, Living with Addiction*. 3rd Edition, Bainbridge Island, Washington: Mac Publishing, 1979.

Conyers, Beverly. *Addict in the Family: Stories of Loss, Hope, and Recovery*. Hazelden, Minnesota: Hazelden Foundation, 2003.

Fewell, Christine Huff and Shulasmith Straussner and Lala Ashenberg. *Impact of Substance Abuse on Children and Families: Research and Practice Implications*. Binghamton, NY: Hawthorn Press, Oct. 26, 2006.

Fine, Carla. *No Time to Say Goodbye: Surviving the Suicide of a Loved One*. Main Street Books, 1997.

Gardner, Anne. *Bipolar Strong: An Empowering Collection by and for Teens and Adults with Bipolar Disorder, Depression and*

Other Neurological Brain Disorders: or "Hidden Disabilities." Xlibris Corporation, 2008.

Kubler-Ross, Elizabeth and David Kessler. *On Grief and Grieving*. New York: Scribner, 2005.

Miller, Angelyn, MA. *The Enabler: When Helping Hurts the Ones You Love*. Tuscon: Wheatmark Publishing, 1999.

Moe, Jerry, MA. *Understanding Addiction and Recovery Through a Child's Eyes: Hope, Help, and Healing for Families*. Deerfield Beach, FL: Health Communication Inc, Nov. 1, 2007.

Waldron, I. *Increased prescribing of Valium, Librium, and other drugs--an example of the influence of economic and social factors on the practice of medicine*. National Center for Biotechnology Information, U.S. National Library of Medicine Rockville Pike, Bethesda MD.

Whitfield, Charles L. *Healing the Child Within: Discovery and Recovery for Adult Children of Dysfunctional Families*. Deerfield Beach, FL: Health Communications, Inc.: April 1, 1987.

Young, William P. *The Shack*. Los Angeles: Windblown Media, 2007.

Web Pages (Active as of July, 2010)

Berger, Lawrence M.; Osborne, Cynthia. "Parental Substance Abuse and Child Well-being: Does it matter which parent has the problem or if they live with the child?," University of Wisconsin. Madison, Wisconsin: March 1, 2009. http://ideas.repec.org

Child Welfare Information Gateway. "Parental Drug Use as Child Abuse: State Statutes," 2009. www.childwelfare.gov

Sheridan, Glyn. "How Does Parental Drug Abuse Affect Children & Teens?," 2010. www.ehow.com

Hitti, Miranda. "Study: Millions of U.S. Kids Living with a Substance-Abusing Adult," March 30, 2005. www.WebMD.com

Limatta, Michael. "Helping Children from Addicted and Dysfunctional Families," *Alcoholics Victorious*, www.alcoholicsvictorious.org

National Association for Children of Alcoholics, www.nacoa.org and www.nacoa.net

National Council on Child Abuse and Family Violence. "Parental Substance Abuse A Major Factor in Child Abuse and Neglect," 2010. www.nccafv.org/parentalsubstanceabuse

Clearinghouse Web Sites (Active as of July, 2010)

http://www.samhsa.gov/children/

http://www.brainyquote.com/quotes/authors/v/virginia_satir.html

http://dictionary.reference.com/browse/regret

http://www.bartleby.com/quotations/

http://www.quoteland.com

Acknowledgments

Without the encouragement of my spouse Gail my painful journey toward hope would be little more than a written exercise in catharsis. It was her wisdom that believed others could benefit from the life Jenny and I shared. More than anything, I am thankful she has joyfully shared life with me for over 35 years and handled my deep pain with loving care. She has made my pain and joy her own, and I only pray that I do the same for her. She is in every way my soul-mate.

My two daughters, Heather and Paige, and granddaughter Kamdyn have been a necessary source of joy for me as I walked through the depressive recollections in this story. They have always been my delight and have empowered me to believe in hope in life's darkest moments.

I am at a loss to thank my editor A. Louise Staman. Her love of words and heartfelt expression have taught me the agony and ecstasy of writing. She has allowed my story to become a meaningful part of her own life. She has handled my every word with such care that I remain deeply touched. I thank God that my writing found her hands and heart. She is a writer's editor. Her passion, unwillingness to settle for anything other than my best, and rich humanity earn my greatest respect.

I am thankful for Chris, Penny, Robin and Gladys for the loving care they offered Jenny. They were often the balm for Jenny's deep wounds. I am especially thankful for Gladys, and for becoming my Dad's best friend, and a matriarch for our family. For the first time, in Gladys he found a wife who gave more than she asked.

I miss being able to express my earnest love and admiration for my father. The years have allowed my admiration for him to grow. He taught me what it meant to love one's spouse unconditionally.

For seven fellow clergy, Dr. Rick Lanford, Dr. Robert Beckum, Rev. Steve Waldorf, Dr. Jay Harris, Rev. Wayne Racz, Dr. Derek McAleer, and Dr. Edwin Chase, called "The Order," I am greatly indebted. Their honest faith and humanity have allowed me to unashamedly laugh and cry. They have defined for me the real meaning of fellowship in Christ, each being a priest to me in his own way. Their service for Jenny at the Methodist Home for Children and Youth walked us through utter despair with grace beyond understanding.

I remain deeply respectful and thankful for those family members and friends who were always there in some of the most difficult times. The Paul and Dot Eames, Thad and Bobbie Davis, Woody and Peggy Woodward families are fixtures in my memories and heart. I was and am blessed with kind, good-hearted aunts and uncles on both sides of the family, but none more so than My Uncle Fred and Aunt Joyce Murdock of Memphis who modeled a loving family for Jenny and me.

I am especially indebted to Dr. Joe Morgan and Dr. Brian Griner for the compassionate healing ministries they offer in the community and beyond. I hold both in high esteem and great respect. I am also grateful to Judge H. Arthur McLane. For years he has represented justice in this community. No one has occupied the bench with more dignity, grace and steadfast character than Judge McLane. He stands tall in my eyes and I will forever look up to him as one of the finest men I have known in my life and ministry.

Finally, I will never be able to express the important role The Methodist Home for Children and Youth has played in my life and Jenny's. They represent the best of the best in care for children caught in the lifestyle Jenny and I lived.

God has ensured that love has always been present, and continues to birth every good gift in my life. It is in the hope of Christ that I face the future believing "all things will work toward the good."

Gail and Craig Rikard

About the Author

Dr. D. Craig Rikard and his wife Gail have led busy lives together. Craig has been a United Methodist Clergyman for over thirty-two years. Gail has taught preschool and presently works in a physician's office. Together they have two daughters and one granddaughter. With Gail's help Craig has earned three post-graduate degrees in theology and marriage and family therapy. They love music and traveling. Perhaps their greatest shared love is that of theater, often visiting Broadway. Although much of their journey through life has been shared, each values the individuality of the other. Gail is energized by group activities, whereas Craig experiences renewal and peace standing alone in a mountain stream fly-fishing. Their shared faith and love, enlivened by their differences, have led to 36 years of marriage.